T0221614

How a
24-YEAR-OLD
Achieved
FINANCIAL
FREEDOM

A GUIDE TO HELPING YOU OBTAIN
MASSIVE WEALTH AT A YOUNG AGE

JASON J. LEE

A SAVIO REPUBLIC BOOK
An Imprint of Post Hill Press
ISBN: 979-8-88845-439-8
ISBN (eBook): 979-8-88845-440-4

How a 24-Year-Old Achieved Financial Freedom:
A Guide to Helping You Obtain Massive Wealth at a Young Age
© 2024 by Jason J. Lee
All Rights Reserved

Cover Design by Conroy Accord

This is a work of nonfiction. All people, locations, events, and situations are portrayed to the best of the author's memory.

posthillpress.com
New York • Nashville
Published in the United States of America

1 2 3 4 5 6 7 8 9 10

This book is dedicated to Kristyna
and my two dogs: Poppy and Daisy.
For keeping me happy and sane through it all.

CONTENTS

Chapter One

MY STORY

I want to take you on a journey. A journey from poor to free. This journey starts on the vibrant streets of Seoul, South Korea. The bustling capital is a captivating blend of ancient traditions and modern innovation. This city, located in the middle of the Korean Peninsula, has over 10 million residents and is a diverse and lively place. The sounds of honking motorbikes, hurried people, and car horns produce a symphony of chaos in Seoul. This is where I was born and lived my first seven years.

Growing up in Seoul provided me with a powerful Korean work ethic very early on. It filled my life with toil, persistence, and a blend of experiences that have formed who I am today. The educational system in Seoul was challenging. I learned about both the Korean and English language. At age six, I was doing equations like multiplication and division. After school, you would find me playing soccer and piano. From morning until 8 p.m., something always kept me occupied. Finally, at seven or eight in the evening, I could head home for dinner. This schedule embedded within me an intense habit of working long hours from a very young age.

When I was four years old, we moved into a different apartment. Looking back, it was a terrible and rough neighborhood. The apartment was old and run down, and the neighborhood had telltale signs of a slum. The playground was old, worn out, and dirty. As a kid, I didn't understand this. However, even though I was young, I could sense the disparities between my life and those of my peers. I saw that our living situations were not equal; my uncle was a successful doctor in Korea and his living situation was significantly better than ours. My grandparents' neighborhood in Seoul was much nicer as well.

My father retired from the US Army when I was seven, and I was yanked from the life I'd known in Korea. After Dad's retirement, we moved to the United States. We settled in Clayton, California, near our family. My dad's family—grandparents, aunt, and uncle—were all living just ten minutes away. I'd gone from the chaotic energy of a busy city to small-town America, which was quite the shock to my system. I was used to living in a city where everyone looked like me. Now, I was living in a small suburb where nobody looked like me. I was different, and the kids in my area didn't like that.

Navigating from elementary school through high school was full of challenges. There was a decent language barrier when I arrived in California and started school. Despite having learned some English in Korea, we only spoke Korean in our household. It wasn't that the other kids were smarter than me, I just didn't have the same communication skills they did. I had trouble making friends and connecting with people. I dealt with racism and bullying a lot. Sixth grade is when the bullying hit its peak, and I got in trouble a few times a week for fighting other kids or acting out in class. But things started to change in high school.

When I started playing sports in high school, I felt like I was a part of a group and had some structure. It was also where the work ethic I had picked up in Korea really paid off for the first time. I was short (still am), slow, and had no muscle when I got into high school. Some of my friends in middle school challenged me to try out for the football team, so I did. I was terrible in the first year. But I learned the game, got some experience under my belt, and finally made some good friends.

To become tougher and more athletic, I started wrestling. This helped me build toughness and grow some muscle. Then, I ran track to get faster. I improved my athletic ability and became a starter for the team when I returned the next year. Everyone was confused about how I had improved over the off-season, but I knew it was because I had worked my ass off. The rest of high school was a great time for me. In my sophomore year, I started playing rugby, and that was my first true passion. It was all I could think about. I studied the game every day, watched YouTube videos of the best players in the world, practiced everyday, encouraged my friends to play, and became extremely good at it. The summer after I graduated, I played for a team in Moraga, and I scored thirteen tries in one of our tournaments (similar to a touchdown if you know football but not rugby). I helped lead us to a championship that weekend. I felt on top of the world when I played the game. I wanted to play college rugby at San Diego State, but I suffered eight different concussions in high school. The physician at SDSU said if I got another concussion, I could potentially die or become a vegetable for life. That news killed me inside because all I cared about was sports, and it had become my lifeline—the one thing I cared about and where I held my personal identity.

This left me feeling lost when it came time to deal with the whole new world I was entering in San Diego. It was the first time I had been away from my close family, and none of my close friends from high school came down to San Diego, so I felt very anxious and alone when I first arrived at the dorms.

My parents thought it'd be a good idea for me to go down the pre-med route, kinesiology or biology. They wanted me to take the courses needed to apply to medical school. The advice my mom gave me was largely due to my aunt. She and her husband were dentists and anesthesiologists who made a *lot* of money. I remember every holiday when I was a kid, my little brother and I would be excited to see them because each time we saw our aunt and grandparents they would give us a present in a little white envelope. Each envelope would have somewhere in between one hundred to five hundred dollars in it. The little naive kid I was never realized how embarrassing it was for my parents. They would give my parents money as well because they knew money was a problem for us. Fast forward to today, I definitely realize why that was a huge blow to my mom's ego.

Meanwhile, my dad was a security guard and worked a lot of overtime to make extra money for us to get by. My mom took odd jobs to get us out of financial instability while I was growing up. She was even an entrepreneur herself! When I was ten years old, she started her own smoothie store in Castro Valley. I remember vividly how much she struggled during that time. She dealt with some crazy customers that complained to her, had to fire employees, had to deal with my younger brother and I when we were young and annoying to deal with, and so much more. Unfortunately, that business failed after a couple of years. After the business closed down, my mom's struggles only got worse...

The first year after her business failed, she worked at the mall at a retail store, and she hated it. Then, she quit and jumped over to a different company working in retail again, and she hated it. Then, she started working at a local gym in Walnut Creek as a janitor, and she hated it. Then, she started working as a janitor at the building my dad works at, and she *hated it*. This is why I don't understand why she ended up sticking to this career full time...because eventually she started her own cleaning business where she still—to this day—cleans houses for clients. She is the highest tier you can get on TaskRabbit. I have gifted my mom a significant amount of money and bought her a cash flowing rental property in Oceanside, but she still works her tail off...

I remember one night very vividly when I was in high school where she came home from an extremely hard and long day of cleaning. She was exhausted and thought everyone was asleep because it was past 10 p.m. I heard her crying heavily, talking to herself saying how miserable she was and how she didn't want to be alive anymore. That night happened several times after that. My mom absolutely hates what she does, and her parents even shamed her for it. But, she won't stop no matter how much I tell her to because she says she has nothing else to do. It gives her a sense of purpose. She always tells me how she would be more depressed if she stopped working. I have the ability to retire her, but she says it will kill her. Being a caring son, all I can think about is her breathing a bunch of bad chemicals everyday and having back problems from bending over so much. That shit is manual labor! It fucking sucks! It kills me that my mom found purpose in that. She also doesn't have any friends, and neither does my dad. It's only getting worse now as I write this because my parents are in the middle of getting a divorce. I may look like I have it all together on social media and no problems, but that is the furthest thing from the truth. One of the biggest problems I deal with today is that my parents primarily speak Korean. My mom's English isn't the best. I live five hundred miles away where I only speak English on a daily basis. So the communication between my parents and I is fading more and more as the years go by. I need to spend more time on Duolingo.

Watching my parents struggle created a lot of trauma for me around the subject of money. I watched my parents have difficulty making ends meet, as they were unable to predict if the next paycheck would be enough. Being young and naïve, I was oblivious to our financial situation and what it meant. I just knew I never wanted to be in that same predicament. Almost every big fight that my parents had when I was young was about money.

I had no idea what I wanted to do when I went to San Diego State for my first semester of college. Using the success of my aunt and uncle as a guide, I took my parents' suggestions and declared a major in the pre-med field.

I was devoted to my major and made sure I put in the effort, so I could make my family proud. For the first two and a half years, I was in the library all the time…. After joining a fraternity in my second semester, I managed to have a social life, made lots of friends, and had the full San Diego State college experience. But when it came to lectures, studying, and doing projects, I was absolutely miserable. I didn't want to do it, and I didn't understand why I felt this way. I felt like a robot just running through a system set up by society. I felt like there was no way out, and that this was the only way to graduate and make money in the future.

I started becoming increasingly curious about other potential paths at the start of my junior year. I started asking every wealthy friend I knew what their parents did for work. I saw the emerging trend that many of their parents built their wealthy by starting their own business, being in real estate investing, or working in finance. And it got me thinking a lot. During summer breaks I had worked for Nordstrom as a sales associate in Walnut Creek, CA. That was where I got my first taste of commission-based sales. If we didn't sell shoes, we made minimum wage, and I did not want to make minimum wage. These experiences got me thinking, "Should I change my path?" But, me being my conscientious self, I was too scared to change my major. I was too scared to go through with anything. Then came the worst semester of my life—all because of organic chemistry.

Before this class started, I was actually excited about premed because I was so close to being done with all of the classes that I hated! Everyone told me that after organic chemistry, that I would be fine! Then, the lectures, weekly quizzes, and tests started. I became more depressed than I'd ever been in my life. I was just drawing octagons and shapes all day and trying to combine carbon and nitrogen for seemingly no reason. I knew we'd never use it in real life, and I felt like it was the stupidest thing to waste my time on. Why do I need to be doing this if I eventually want to heal people? When I see a patient at my practice, am I going to show them stupid diagrams of molecules that they don't care about? Hell no! Who does that? Nobody!

This was the moment when I finally realized that school is a complete and utter scam, and I needed to get the fuck out of here as soon as possible.

Surprisingly, I made it to finals week. When I was studying my ass off, my friends and I got tickets to go to the Louis The Child concert in the San Diego area to take a break. I decided to try something that I had never tried before: psilocybin. I had heard this plant could act as a powerful medicine and had profound effects for opening up your mind to new possibilities. And boy were they right! This night completely changed my life forever.

I am telling you right now, if I didn't have this experience during my last week of my first semester junior year, I wouldn't be sitting here writing this book today. This book is me, Jason Lee, trying to help a college kid in their early twenties. I know how miserable societal pressure and family pressure can be. For some of you, breaking free might seem impossible, but if the most average kid like me can do it, so can you. Keep reading.

Anyways, I was a menace at the concert. I built up the confidence somehow to hit on my crush at the time (she rejected me, didn't care whatsoever). In the Uber on the way home, I was singing the entire way while my friends were laughing at my intoxicated self. I'd never sung in my life in front of anyone. Then I went into our house, and suddenly, I started yelling the craziest epiphanies that I realized in the car.

I started giving speeches that night to my friends about how our parents are holding us back and how we have so much more potential than we think. "School is a *waste of time!*" "Call my friend, we are about to start a business!" "I am about to get rich from bitcoin, let's go!" Those are 1 percent of the crazy things I said that night. I gave speeches to my friends yelling: "We can't let others control our lives! We can do whatever the fuck we want!" I was going on rants about this all night, and most people thought I was crazy, but at least the stranger in the Uber who rode with us was vibing with what I was saying.

After that night, my life has not been the same. In fact, after that fateful turning point, my life took a complete 180. After I took my finals the next couple of day, I changed my major. I joined various societies and clubs on campus, including the Financial Planning Association and the Real Estate Society (RES).

People ask me all the time, "How did you get into real estate?" I always keep my answer to myself, since it is not PG or considered professional in the real world. The craziest part of it all is that I don't even know why I decided to join the Real Estate Society. My subconscious mind just knew there were treasures to be found in the real estate career, and boy was my gut right!

On top of that, at the first event I decided to sign up for after joining the society, I met the mentor who changed my life! Thank you Brian and Kevin for taking a chance on me. You have taught me a lot of what I know, and without you I would not be here today.

At the networking event, they matched twenty professionals with twenty students and spread out among twenty tables. We had short two-minute conversations with each of the professionals like it was a game of speed dating. I had totally bombed my first six conversations with the professionals, and I felt more insecure every time we changed tables. Luckily, on my seventh conversation I had the conversation that would change my life forever. I met my old mentor Brian.

We hit it off at the RES networking event, and he invited me to his office for a follow-up interview. I feel like he was the only one there that day who was there with one mission: to hire some motivated young guns like myself.

The next week I went into his office feeling scared and nervous as hell. I thought he was going to grill me with tough questions that I had no idea how to answer. I didn't even know what an escrow or a purchase agreement was at that time. I knew absolutely nothing about real estate during that stage in my life.

When the interview started in Brian's conference room, I was actually pleasantly surprised. He didn't ask one thing about my resume or work experience! The entire time he pitched his company and why I should join. He liked that I was an athlete. He told me that athletes do great in real estate because they have the competitive spirit built into them. From that interview, I got hired as an intern. He just saw something in me and wanted to hire me.

I thought, "Oh, I wonder what my base pay and my hourly wage will be as an intern." That was when Brian dropped a bomb—there was no hourly wage, there was no base salary. He said, "You're just going to be learning, and you're going to be hitting the phones in order to find a lead. And whenever you find a lead, and you close a lead, that's when you get paid. You only get paid for what you kill. If you don't make sales, you don't get paid."

That's why he didn't ask me many questions about my resume! It would cost him nothing to hire me. I looked him in the eye and squeaked out a very nervous, "Great." Everything in my head was telling me, "Don't do this. It's a stupid idea." I had less than $500 in my Chase Bank account that day. It made absolutely no sense to take this job instead of something that would put money in that account in one or two weeks.

But something in my gut told me, "If all these guys are extremely successful, making multiple six figures to over a million dollars a year, why can't I do it too? I'm going to get there. These guys all have successful businesses. This is what my future's going to look like." And for some reason, I shook his hand and took that job. Since that day, my life has never been the same.

I'm not here to tell you it was an easy road because it was absolute hell for the first six months. This is where that young, poor boy from Korea at the start of the journey helped form who I am. That fiery, motivated spirit inside me who had trained himself to put in hours of labor came to my rescue once more. I was still studying at school, but without a job, I lacked the funds I needed. I had to get a job. I took a tutoring job where I tutored statistics once or twice a week. They paid me $600 a month to host eight sessions a week.

To make ends meet, I also started running social media ad campaigns for a local coffee shop and a musician named Will Clark. They each paid me $500 a month. I was living off $1,600 a month and attending school full-time while interning at this company for two or three days a week. I was working seven days a week, trying to get through school.

Finally, summer came along, and this is where I saw some forward progress. I got my real estate license over the summer. I was working two days a week at the real estate office and doing the social media thing. I also worked serving poolside at the Sheraton by the San Diego Airport three or four times a week to help me get through. Between all of these, I made three or four grand a month while also learning real estate daily.

After I got my real estate license, going into my senior year of college fall of 2018, I worked Monday, Wednesday, and Friday all day, twelve hours a day. I was working thirty-six to forty hours a week in those three days. On Tuesdays and Thursdays, I stacked my classes all day long to where I had six classes, an hour and a half, back to back to back to back. I had changed my major late in my college career, so I had to take more classes than the norm to graduate on time. It was awful, but not *nearly* as bad as organic chemistry.

My roommate and one of my best friends, Blake Laurin, can attest I was never at home. It was an exhausting year. But I had worked this hard and knew I had to do it because I wanted to beat the system. I wanted to give back to my parents so badly and do something big, so I put in extra effort during senior year while most people were just skating by trying to get as much partying in before they graduate and go into the real world. My entire senior year, I felt like I was in the real world already with how much I was working, that when I graduated it was very anti-climactic. For three months, I worked relentlessly, making 150 cold calls a day, being rejected dozens of times daily, and speaking with folks that did *not* want to talk to me at all. I kept getting the phone slammed in the face, and people yelled to "take them off my list." Finally, in November, I made a break-through: I got my first listing.

I finally secured a meeting with a motivated seller and got the listing signed for a fourplex in east San Diego. I was thrilled and elated. I'd just gotten my first listing after six months of struggling without a salary or hourly wage. It got so hard and the thought of giving up almost crossed my mind. But now that

I had this new listing, I could sense the momentum finally going in a positive direction for the first time in my life! I was on top of the world! Then a week later, all my momentum crashed. My client's father unexpectedly passed away. He was unprepared and didn't have a family trust set up for his family, which meant the property (my first listing!) was going to probate.

Probate is a curse word in real estate. Once a property is passed on to probate, it is up to the government—be it the state, county, or municipality—to administer the estate. This process can take an extensive amount of time to complete, with some cases taking years to finalize. When my broker explained all this, I walked out to my car and started crying my ass off— truly bawling my eyes out on the drive home. I didn't talk to anyone that whole night, and I told myself that I would quit the next day. I told myself real estate was not for me. I thought, "I'm just going to get a job. My parents were right. My friends were right. I took too big of a risk. I'm stupid for doing all this stuff. I'm a complete and utter failure."

And at this moment in my life I realized that failure and success live right next to each other. This story is the biggest inflection point of my life. As soon as I woke up that next day, I knew that I shouldn't quit. I knew I should keep going. After the initial shock passed, I realized how much I had learned and the progress I had made, so that's when I motivated myself to keep chugging. I kept saying to myself, "I am getting closer. If this shit was easy, then everyone would be rich."

Within a month or so, a miracle happened. the property fell out of probate, the owner (now the son) had control of the property, and I got my listing back. I sold that property a couple of months after. Then, just two months after that, I closed two more deals. Before I graduated from college, I had five deals under my belt. I had made almost $100,000!

I had more money in my bank account than I ever had in my life in a relatively short time. I immediately paid off my student loans after I graduated. I was now debt-free, hungrier than ever to do more deals, and I knew I was going to succeed.

After I graduated, my career exploded because now I had seven days a week to focus on real estate and nothing else for the first time in my life. Serving at a restaurant, running Facebook ads for coffee shops/artists, studying for tests in school, and being a part time tutor was slowly killing my mental health. For the first time in my life, I could focus on one thing and one thing only: becoming the best real estate agent I could be. So, from 2019 to 2020, that's all I did.

It takes sacrifice, adversity, loneliness, sleepless nights, anxiety, and overcoming self-doubt and anxiety to make it. I realized that when I graduated, I didn't have any friends anymore because I hadn't kept in touch with any of them or hung out with anyone on the weekend for a very long time besides my few friends who ended up moving out of San Diego. When I graduated, I was a loner. To save all the money I could, I rented a little studio loft apartment that was like two hundred square feet to save money and I just worked all damn day in the office. Why need a fancy place when I am never there? In 2019, I ended the year with twelve deals, making over $150,000 in my first full year in real estate. Then in 2020, the pandemic hit.

This is the epitome of what it takes to get out of the system because even when the pandemic hit, I still had the courage, persistence, and discipline to show up every day, make those calls, and keep going. I kept talking to people and meeting my clients no matter what, whether on Zoom or via phone, and I did whatever I could to stay on top of their minds.

Even when nothing was happening for three months, I was still going to the office every day, and that's when my business truly exploded. That's what it takes to get out of the system. You have to grind harder than everyone else. You have to work harder and smarter. No matter how much effort you put into a job that only pays eighteen dollars per hour, your compensation remains the same. You could work even harder the following day, but it won't make a difference. Your yearly earnings will be capped. This is why you have to work hard and smart. Be smart, and work in a career where your income can't be capped by anyone but yourself. This is the biggest reason why I beat the system. I did this very early in my life.

There is no ceiling in real estate. When you are a real estate agent, you are the owner of your own business. The real estate agents who fail are the ones who think they have a new job. It's not a job, it's a new business you're starting. Starting a business is the fastest way to achieve time freedom, and real estate is the best business to be in.

As a real estate entrepreneur, I was able to make over $600,000 in 2020. In April of 2021, I took another huge leap of faith and started JLM Real Estate, while simultaneously starting my podcast, *Get Out of The System*. The same year, I personally bought fourteen properties and increased my net worth from one million to about five million dollars. My company also did well, with about $1.6 million in net commission income that year alone. And in 2022, I made over $2 million in commissions net in my pocket, and today in 2023 my net worth is over

$10 million, I own 125 units in San Diego, and the real estate portfolio is worth over $50 million.

I was obsessed with learning about investing in real estate, constantly asking investors questions about how they did it, and picking up tips and techniques from my clients who already had experience as investors. I also saved all of the commissions that I earned to use for future investments. This meant not eating out, going out to the bars, wasting my time with people who didn't think like me, and instead just investing my time and money every waking hour. I ended up buying my first property in 2020, made over a million dollars on it, and kept rolling my profits over and over and over again. Living frugally and reinvesting everything is how I became financially free exceptionally quickly.

But it didn't start out this way for me. And odds are, it didn't start out for you like this either. The moment you were born, you were put into this box: elementary school, then middle school, high school, and eventually college (for some). Your teachers were stuck in the same loop as well, never learning how to provide a proper financial education to their students, the higher ups telling them to teach kids subjects that will never help prepare them for the real world. Most teachers robotically teach the youth from textbooks that are outdated and useless in today's world.

Nothing I learned in my sixteen years of being in school applied to becoming successful in my personal life and business life. In school, we are not taught anything of value that can help us develop our creativity, become entrepreneurs, or grow as individuals. Sitting in a chair for eight hours a day while your posture gets worse and your attention span dwindles is the worst way for kids to learn. The intelligent kids who lash out and don't like doing that are labeled as kids with severe "ADHD." To make things worse, these students are prescribed pills that they call "medication," and ruin their creative minds. This is the entire educational system from preschool to high school: it destroys kids' brains instead of helping them grow.

After high school, our society puts pressure on you to go to college. Same shit, but only worse because you don't necessarily have to attend classes in college. It's way easier to cheat and the lecturers are even more boring and less engaging because now there are five hundred people in a classroom instead of twenty people in a classroom. You're on your phone all class with no engagement in the subject. Our college years are a period often riddled with drugs, alcohol, and reckless behavior, which can have a detrimental effect on the brain. Not to mention if you're in debt or your parents are footing the bill, four years of your life have been squandered.

But if you stick out, you can walk across the stage, and then what? You attend job fairs by the time you're a third or fourth-year student, where you learn how to gain an internship at a large organization or get hired for a starting position in an established corporation. Congratulations, you're now in corporate America. Or even worse, you fucked off for the entire four years, and you spent your parents' money (or your money), you're in over $30,000 worth of debt, and you have no leads on jobs. You didn't learn to network, so you're just working as a barista at Starbucks. I've seen that happen before to real people, and it's the saddest thing. They invested time and energy in their college education, but it didn't amount to anything real. Their lectures were of no use in the outside world. It's a sad truth. It's all about *who* you know, not *what* you know.

Unless you networked in college, met people, and made relationships, college was a complete waste of time for you. Let's be honest, how many people can remember three things they learned in lectures in college? Not that many people could list three off the top of their heads. And one of the saddest stories I can tell you is I sat in some entrepreneurship classes, and at the end of the class, the teachers were promoting internships at big companies and encouraging people to go to job fairs. I mean, how sad is that? You're teaching an entrepreneurship class and telling kids to get jobs. That just proves that college is a total waste of time and money. None of it made any sense to me.

It only gets worse after that. You're still stuck in the system, of course. And now the system, corporate America, teaches you how to be a worker for someone else. Now you're just a drone working at a desk for forty-plus years, maybe fifty, and then you retire. Hopefully, when that happens, you have a pension, a 401(k) to live paycheck to paycheck, and then you die. You slowly deteriorate your mind for the next twenty years of your life in retirement by watching TV all day, getting pissed off at CNN or Fox News, and then you pass away. Good job. You've successfully made it through a normal life.

This is the fucking system. This is why I am writing this book. This is the average life of an American who works and lives through the system. That is what life is like for 99 percent of people in America, and it is what pisses me off every single day when I wake up. There are so many people who are just stuck as drones, like they're robots. The US encourages people to be part of a conformist society, where the only way of making

18

it is to become a worker rather than an innovator or risk-taker. People are discouraged from trying anything that involves taking chances. They don't show you how to invest because if you invest, you will become free, and the corporations don't want that. They want you to work daily to make money for the Amazons and the Teslas of the world.

There's a way out of the system, but you must take a different path than you've been taught. The road less traveled is becoming an entrepreneur and investing in hard assets. That is something that 99.9 percent of the world does not do. You have to recognize what it is that motivates you. What are you proud of investing time and effort into? When I go to work every day, I am fired up when I start working on Monday. I am excited to get up, go to the gym, meet with my team, train them, and do deals. We work as a family, and everyone there is excited to get going and work on their business.

We all have individual businesses; I teach them and provide support to run their own business inside of our company umbrella. That's the beauty of real estate. You have to find a career that you're either passionate about, or if you can't do that, you have to have a career where no one can control your income. With no restrictions in place, you could make an unlimited amount of money. There are no limits to your earnings, no pre-established salary, and no one regulating how you should spend your time.

That is how you get ahead of 99 percent of the population, especially if you are reading this in your early twenties. From there, just like me, you want to save the money you make from sales and use that money to buy real estate. Buy cash flowing assets that create residual income, properties that work hard for you even when you're sleeping. That way, even when you're not working, it will help you retire and maximize your net worth as soon as possible. This is true wealth. True wealth is found by investing. This book shows you the path out of the system and into the life you want step by step. I don't like reading books where authors just mention big concepts and motivate you. If you follow the step-by-step process in this book, I will guarantee that you will be financially free and worth multiple millions sooner than you can imagine. If you came up to me five years ago and told me that I would be worth $10 million by the time I was twenty-six years old, I would have slapped you across the face. "Don't fuck with me like that!"

But here's the kicker: you could do what I do for forty-plus years, and if you don't invest a dime of what you make, you'll never truly be wealthy. You become rich from what you own, not from what you do.

If I would not have invested a dime of what I made and just spent it on cars, food, and partying, and paid an insane amount of taxes, I would barely be a millionaire. I live in California, so the IRS takes 37 percent of my income being in the highest tax bracket, and then California takes 12.1 percent of my income when I file as an S-Corp. In 2021, I netted over $1.5 million. If I didn't invest in real estate, I would have paid around $750,000 in income tax…. Makes me want to throw up.

Invest your money as soon as possible into assets that go up in value over time, create wealth for you, and generate cash flow. That is how you achieve financial freedom. That is how you get out of the matrix.

As I write this book, I'm making well over six figures a year in cash flow from my properties to where I never have to work again. Tell me, would you rather retire at age twenty-six or at sixty-five? Because if I really wanted to, I could stop working right now, but I love what I do. I love helping people win. I love real estate. I love making a positive impact. I will continue to pursue my dreams and work hard because I have found my talent. Now, I use it to help others get out of the system, which has lit a bigger fire inside me.

I've trained agents on how to make money as an investor, and now they have the roadmap to becoming financially free. My top producer, Ryan, made over $200,000 in the first couple years of his career. That's considerably more than a standard job coming right out of college. He's looking to buy his first multi-unit property where he can live and rent out the other units. That's building true wealth because he knows how to do that now. He has the knowledge to buy a property the right way, to buy a good deal where it makes sense financially. I've given him and my team the roadmap to retire, probably within the next five years, if they choose to work hard to obtain freedom.

In the next chapters, you'll learn exactly what I did to become financially free at age twenty-six. If you are reading this book, it means that you don't want to work for the rest of your life. You don't want to be a corporate drone until you're sixty-five to seventy years old. You don't want to work at Walmart when you're seventy-five years old because you ran out of retirement funds. Time is not on your side, period. Life is too fucking short. Think about how fast the last twelve months have gone by in your life and what you accomplished or didn't accomplish. Time is moving quickly, and your time on this earth is finite. It's very small compared to when Earth "was born" (4.6 billion years ago). Google that shit.

You have to take advantage of your life now. You have to create financial freedom and time freedom now. You have to create autonomy where you can do whatever you want, whenever you want, as fast as possible so that you can spend time with your loved ones, create new relationships, follow your true passions, and travel. Doing what you want is the ultimate goal of life. That is true freedom. And if you are forced to punch in a clock every single day to make money and pay your bills, you are confined in an invisible jail cell within the system.

If you are okay with living a life like the 99 percent of the world does, then return this book. It's not for you. It won't help you, and you don't need it. But, if you want to live an extraordinary life and truly have an impact on the world during this short, precious life we have, keep reading.

My mentor told me that once you are twenty-one years old, it feels like the halfway point in your life because time really starts to move faster than ever after that age. Why? Because we get into a mindless job and a routine. How do you want to spend the short amount of time you have?

Chapter Two

WHY TODAY?

B efore I dive deeper into the benefits and the how-tos of investing in real estate, if you have no money right now, email me at jason@jlmcre.com. If you are broke, the fastest way to get your money is to become a badass multi-family real estate agent. Not only can you make six figure commissions, but you will also learn the game. You will learn the ins and outs of how to analyze properties, find great properties, and create relationships with billionaires. The opportunities are endless. Contact me; the window might be closed already if you waited too long.

All of the seasoned investors who have been in the game for twenty-plus years that I've spoken to shared the same opinion: if they could do it all over again, they would have invested in real estate sooner. They all wish they bought more in their early years. Most of them regretted not taking bigger risks.

Here's the thing, the sooner you invest in a property, the more time you have for it to compound and generate you wealth. So *now* is the perfect opportunity to become a real estate investor. Time in the game is your biggest ally in the real estate game.

Real estate provides a greater range of advantages than any other kind of investment—it's not comparable. By starting today, you will be able to take advantage of these benefits much quicker. Real estate provides cash flow, appreciation, tax benefits (IRS calls it depreciation), and principal paydown (paying down your loan with your tenants' rent checks to you).

It's never too late to begin investing in real estate; regardless of your age, you can start learning and building up your portfolio. I've seen several successful investors, with $250 million worth of property who got to that point with no money to begin with. I've also met people starting as early as sixteen years old. Real estate is for everyone. The key is having an abundance mindset, not a limited one; the opportunities are endless.

There are way more than enough properties, and plenty of good deals to go around for everyone out there.

A lot of things that I hear people talking about is, "Oh, well, you're getting the best deals, so there's not enough room for me to get into real estate," "It's too competitive," or, "There's way too much going on and there's way too many people that are fighting for the same property." Contrary to popular belief, there's no shortage of amazing deals out there. I often hear people thinking that because the market is so competitive, they don't stand a chance. That couldn't be further from the truth. In fact, there isn't enough competition, and there are plenty of ways to get creative with real estate by adding value to properties and dominating any niche or asset class you choose.

Think about the sheer variety of properties there are: single-family homes, duplexes, fourplexes, apartment complexes, office buildings, industrial properties, hotels, medical offices, mixed use, raw land, and retail centers. Developers are only building more and as our population grows as well. So the total number of properties increases every year. You may not have even considered golf courses or movie theaters as types of property. Really, there is a seemingly endless selection of unique properties out there you might never have known about.

But the best asset class in real estate is multifamily real estate. I'll be talking about that extensively in the coming chapters, but what I want you to take away from this is that there are so many different avenues to pursue if you want to invest in real estate. Don't be discouraged if you think you're too early or late; anyone can succeed in real estate as long as they put in the time and effort to learn and use that knowledge to make bold decisions.

A key reason to begin today is that the knowledge and market data has never been easier to get. Technology has really leveled the playing field. Before the internet, when knowledge wasn't easily obtainable, many real estate investors wanted to keep the advantages of investing for themselves. The people with established wealth didn't like this change. I remember meeting a client who started talking about how much easier things were before the internet because there was less competition and he could "get every deal he wanted." I hadn't thought of that. It hadn't occurred to me before then, but it's not typical knowledge taught in school or openly discussed in society. The US corporate and educational systems don't encourage the idea of financial freedom through real estate investments; they rather prefer that individuals become dedicated workers and help their businesses succeed. They need you to fit into their mold as an employee.

There are many elderly people out there who have a scarcity mindset and don't want others to know about real estate, but I think it should be celebrated. Just because someone comes from a low-income family and never heard about real estate doesn't mean they can't learn about it. All you need to do is listen to a podcast, watch some YouTube videos (free videos on my channel at @jasonjosephlee), or look up some professionals on social media related to investing in real estate.

Knowledge is truly more accessible than ever. There are thousands of educational podcasts, YouTube videos, LinkedIn pages, and real estate meetups available so that you can network with other investors in your community. In any medium-sized city, there's probably a real estate meetup happening at least once a week.

TikTok is starting to take off as a social media platform, combining aspects of YouTube and Instagram. You can use it to search topics like how to invest in real estate and get helpful results. As a real estate novice, however, be mindful of who you take advice from. Make sure that the person you're following or considering a mentor online is actually engaging in activities related to investing.

There are a lot of fakers out there. There's a lot of people who are just trying to make money off your attention by making videos about what they think they know. In reality, they might own one property and not even be practicing what they preach. I remember last year when I was on YouTube seeing a new creator who has gotten a big following making videos based on fear and insulting other investors and creators on YouTube. He has created very poisonous community. This fake guru called out an intelligent Youtuber for being wrong about the housing market, claiming that home prices were going to fall 40 percent in 2023. It's hilarious writing this now in Q4 of 2023 since home prices are down less than 10 percent. Be careful who you listen to.

For instance, if your goal is to become a successful multi-family investor, you should seek out someone who has already achieved success in that industry. Don't cheat yourself by listening to someone who has not walked the path you want to take. That's one piece of wisdom for somebody just starting out.

There's this couple I know; they said they had wanted to invest in real estate for years but delayed it because they valued "leveling up" their lives more--which meant spending more money on luxury clothes, the nicer cars, the big fancy house, and other extravagant expenses. Their egos were killing them. Even when you're making a lot of money, be careful. It's not about how much you make, it's about how much you keep.

They were always talking about putting their money into real estate, but they kept finding ways to spend it on improving their day-to-day lives. With no savings to spare, they weren't in a position to invest.

And they kept saying, "Oh, we're going to save money and do this," but it just ended up being another vacation or another excuse. "Oh, I'm too busy with the kids," or "I have too much going on and work is so busy. I don't want to think about that right now."

If they had taken the money and rented a nice house, investing the remaining in investment properties instead, they would be so much better off than they are now. The difference would be quite remarkable.

It's safe to assume that their monthly expenses average around $30,000 to $40,000 per month with their mortgage payment comprising half of the total. If they opted to rent a moderately priced house for about $4,000 to $5,000 here in San Diego and invest in two or three properties using the money they would have spent on luxurious living, it wouldn't be difficult for them to cash flow over ten to fifteen grand each month. By doing so, they could easily cover half of their living expenses with the extra income. And if they chose to be more frugal with their spending and focus on long-term investing, they could save even more cash to buy additional investment properties.

There's two parts of the equation because someone who makes $400,000 a year and spends $390,000 a year is no better than someone who makes $30,000 a year and spends $20,000 a year. In the end, for both situations, the net overall in their savings is going to be $10,000.

It's never going to feel perfect. It's always going to feel scary. It's always going to feel like you're overreaching your boundaries or you're doing too much, but that means you're growing. Investing in real estate in the beginning can be uncomfortable. It really tests your mental toughness and your ability to stay calm. Even though real estate is one of the most secure investments you can buy, it still feels scary in the beginning because it's new. Think about a time where you tried something for the first time. Playing new sport, trying a new instrument, stepping up to the tee box your first time golfing, trying out for the talent show at your school, going to your first day at your job. What do those all have in common? You felt uncomfortable because it was new. Real estate is the same way.

When you feel uneasy about a purchase, remind yourself that it's a sign of progress. Buying your first property is a step toward achieving financial independence, and the jitters signify that you're heading in the right direction.

I remember when I finally went into contract on buying my first property...I was *scared shitless*! Even though I ran my numbers one hundred times over, took a photo of every little crevice of the property, hired multiple roofers and plumbers to inspect the property, and studied the sales comparisons in the ZIP code for days, I was still very anxious. Even though I knew I was getting a killer deal on the property, my nerves didn't give me a break. But the second, third, fourth, fifth, and sixth property I bought that year, I was less nervous each time. At this point, I don't even bat an eye when I go into escrow on a new property.

The people that tell you not to invest in real estate—because it's too expensive or overvalued or the market is going to crash—are generally misinformed. Every person I have spoken to that has invested in property for a prolonged period of time have seen their lives transform for the better, and all agree that there is no other way they would have wanted to do it. They have watched as their world has grown exponentially. It's faster and easier, and it's the most effective.

Chapter Three

WHY REAL ESTATE IS THE FASTEST WAY TO BEAT THE SYSTEM

Real estate is the *best* way to break away from the conventional system because anyone, including yourself, can make it work. I've met many individuals who weren't very knowledgeable about real estate yet made it big in this field. This just goes to show how easy it is to get started and be successful with this. It's been done over and over again, proving it's a reliable and viable strategy. If you think you can't do this, think again.

Investing in real estate offers significantly more benefits than other investment opportunities like cryptocurrencies, bonds, stocks, 401(k)s, and Roth IRAs. It delivers a number of advantages that no other asset can provide; it generates cash flow, increases in value (appreciation), offers huge tax deductions (IRS identifies this as depreciation), and your tenants pay off the mortgage for you (principal paydown). This is why multifamily real estate is the best option out of all the other investments out there. No other investment offers all four of those benefits like real estate does. It's not even close!

There's no other investment where you can get this much leverage (a.k.a. this big of a loan) and still be in a very risk-averse position. The stock market can't compete. When you buy stocks on margin (using debt/leverage to buy more stock), it's incredibly more risky than buying real estate with debt on it. There's a reason why the top banks out there—like Chase Bank, Wells Fargo, and Bank of America—love lending on multifamily real estate, but will never lend you any money to buy Amazon or Tesla stock.

All banks seek out real estate investments because they provide the lowest risk option when it comes to loan repayment. Alternative investments, such as companies and stocks, offer a higher risk of non-payment—something banks want to avoid. Banks must make sure their money is being paid back and don't want to get caught in a situation where they have to foreclose on someone's assets.

Banks are more eager to lend money for real estate investments than anything else, especially for multifamily real estate projects. They offer some of the best interest rates, terms, and products available because multifamily properties are one of the safest investments in the world.

Not only that, but multifamily is extremely recession-resistant. Think back to the pandemic in 2020. Many assets that were in pain, especially office and retail. All kinds of properties that require face-to-face contact suffered greatly. But the one type that fared best out of all—better than single family homes, industrial, office, and retail buildings—was multifamily real estate. Apartment complexes were the clear winners during the tough times. Even at the start of 2020, when the severity of COVID wasn't fully realized yet, all of my tenants and all of my clients' tenants were still paying rent. All in all, people were still making money on multifamily real estate despite the pandemic.

As I write this in 2023, a lot of people out there are speculating that multifamily values are going to crash with the rest of commercial real estate because of the fastest interest rate increase in US history. As this logic makes sense, when you buy in a well-located city like San Diego, there isn't much pain or motivation to sell from owners. People here have owned assets in their families for generations, and a lot of the properties are owned with no debt, all equity. This is why prices are barely down still to this day.

I have a friend who owns a very successful spin cycle business here in San Diego, and she couldn't pay her rent to her business landlord. She received the PPP Loan, which was the famous loan that saved all the businesses when COVID hit. My friend's landlord was badly affected since her rent payments were stopped entirely for two years due to the pandemic and the inability of people to use the gym she had in her building.

In the end, my friend left her lease way early with a settlement that was much lower than what was originally agreed upon in the lease. So, in the end, the landlord lost out on over six figures worth of rent. But guess what? My friend never missed one payment when it came to paying her rent at her apartment. People will always prioritize payments to where they live, rather than their office or retail space. This demonstrates just how conservative investing in multifamily real estate can be at even the most challenging times.

While stocks have always been marketed as the common or standard investment for us, it is the lack of control that annoys me about the stock market. When you buy a stock, you're at the mercy of the market and you can't do anything to change how it plays out. For instance, if you buy a stock from Charles Schwab or Robinhood, you simply wait and see what happens; you cannot interact with your stock any further. All you can potentially do is either sell or purchase more shares. Investing in real estate is entirely different, as it gives you remarkable power over the asset. Therefore, I prefer to invest my money in something where I can control my investment rather than sitting on the sidelines as the market dictates my entire future of my investment.

If you're the sole owner of a property, there are several types of renovations you can do to increase its value. For instance, adding parking spaces, installing washer/dryers, and adding other amenities makes it more attractive to potential tenants. You can also build additional dwellings or legally expand the existing size of the units. You can develop more ADUs (accessory dwelling units, a.k.a. stand-alone units). In terms of the physical structure, you can put on a new roof, put in updated windows, make the kitchen and living room bigger, or even add bedrooms and bathrooms with permission from the city. And every single one of these things increases your property's overall market value.

There are so many things you can do to increase the value of a property, and you can't do that with any stock you buy.

The other thing about stocks is that you never know everything about the business you are investing in. Let's say I want to buy Google stock. I don't actually know what's going on inside of Google. What if I bought Google stock right before the day before they laid off thirty thousand employees? I would have no idea until the news came out, right? So, this is where stocks become a sticking point for me: the lack of information and the lack of control. A single negative headline about Google or any company can ruin the price of your stock. That will never happen with real estate. The supply and demand fundamentals of real estate will protect your investment. Real estate is also very illiquid, meaning that as soon as someone wants to sell, it is not a quick process. It takes thirty to ninety days on average to sell a piece of real estate. With stocks, you can sell the stock immediately, which can cause values to come crashing down much faster than real estate.

With real estate, I know everything that's going on. I can know how much properties are selling for in the area just by asking a local real estate broker or pulling the data myself by saying, "I'm going to look at every single property, every single house, or every single apartment complex that was sold in the last year in this specific ZIP code to make sure that I'm not overpaying for the property." Whereas when I buy a stock, I don't know if I'm overpaying. It's a much tougher investment of value and it's much more complicated. With real estate, it's very easy to know if you are getting a good deal or not. If the homes in your area are selling for an average of $1 million and you buy an investment property for $800,000, you just bought a great deal. You're walking into equity on day one. And if there's room to add value, you're walking into even more equity.

If I buy Google stock, I can't call the CEO of Google and say, "Hey, I know your stock's trading at $2,000, but I want to buy the stock for $1,500." They would laugh you off the phone and say, "Never call me again." But if I call a seller of a property and I ask them, "Hey, can I buy your property for $800,000?" (even though the average value of that house is around $1 million) and they say yes because they want to get out quickly or they need to sell fast for whatever reason (or they just don't care because they just want to get their money now), you can do that. There's nothing that's stopping you. It's a free market. That's why real estate is amazing because everything is negotiable in real estate, and it's very unregulated, unlike the stock market. If you do any of that kind of stuff in the stock market, it's called insider trading. But in real estate, it's just negotiating. So, that is the beauty of real estate that I love more than anything else.

So, how do you get started? How do you start reaping the benefits of real estate? How do you find a good deal? How do you find a great property? How do you meet the people that'll direct you the right way? Well, here's how you get started.

This is exactly what I did, and I really want to truly be open about this. The best way to get into real estate is by becoming a real estate professional and being a service provider for investors currently in the market. What I mean by that is to be someone who serves the investors in your area so you can learn from those investors, and then you can learn how to invest in real estate. The best thing you can do to learn about investing in real estate and to create the network you need to succeed is to become a multifamily real estate agent.

If you're in constant contact with real estate investors, it won't be long until you become one. As a real estate agent, broker, property manager, appraiser, lender, or banker talking to investors, you'll learn the business quicker than anybody else, if you network with and work for them on a daily basis.

The fastest way to learn real estate if you are young and inexperienced is by being a real estate agent. If you are still at a W2 job that you hate, or you're coming right out of college, get your real estate license as soon as possible. Email me if you need help with this process: jason@jlmcre.com.

As a multifamily real estate agent, you are looking at different deals all day long and communicating with buyers and sellers who are all investors. You can get a firm understanding of how to serve both buyers and sellers. And this makes you a lethal weapon when you want to be a real estate investor because you'll already know the lingo and you know what a good deal is (since you are analyzing properties every day when you are an active real estate professional).

When I first started in the business, I was cold calling for most of the day, which was followed by an hour of going over my leads and analyzing the properties to get a sense of their market value. After doing this for a couple of years, eventually I just knew the San Diego market like the back of my hand. So, after talking with investors and my broker taught me how to invest and shared the knowledge that I'm sharing with you right now, I was ready to buy my first property—I mean, I was so damn ready. I knew exactly what kind of property I wanted to pounce on, and when I found it, I pounced on it right away because I knew it was a great deal. I bought my first deal in 2020 for $630,000, and one year later, it appraised for $2.1 million.

If you want to enter the real estate market right away, becoming a multifamily investments real estate agent is your best bet. It isn't suitable for everyone, but having the right mindset and mentor will help you succeed. Remember, if you become an agent, all of your income will depend on commissions. You eat what you kill. No base salary.

When you're a property manager, appraiser, or lender, you will get a base salary plus commission, usually. But I'm telling you right now, the fastest way to make money and the fastest way to get into real estate as an investor is through stacking up commissions as an agent. Most property managers, appraisers, or lenders are lucky to make six figures in their first couple of years.... As a third-year real estate agent, I netted over $1.5 million in commissions through selling multifamily real estate.

If you're already well established in your career and making a solid income, whether it's in tech sales, medicine, law, or owning a business, then getting a real estate license isn't necessary. There's no reason to switch careers or take on more work since you already have the capacity to invest in a property.

Focus is the most important key to being a successful business person and an investor, and the less things you have on your plate, the better you can focus. So, if you have a successful photography business and you make a lot of money there, don't be a real estate agent. Just focus on making more money as a photographer and invest what you make in real estate on the side. Investing in multifamily real estate can be very passive. It doesn't take up a lot of your time, if you do it right. So, invest in real estate, but also keep making more money in your business if it is successful.

Those are the two fastest ways to get into real estate—either have your own real estate business as a real estate agent or broker or have your own successful business in any other field (it can be in music, golf, selling desks, or any kind of business) and invest in real estate. The fastest way to get out of the system is taking the cash flow from the business and investing it all into real estate. That is how you become financially free. That is exactly how you get out of the system.

But the catch is—and it's very important—you can't do one without the other. You can't just be a real estate agent, you can't just be a business owner, and you can't just be a high-income earner. When you do that, 30 to 50 percent of your income is going to the IRS and the state, depending on where you live. When that much of your money goes to Uncle Sam, it's going to be very hard for you to become wealthy.

The reason why real estate investors become rich so much faster than the average person is because you save a lot of money in taxes by owning real estate. I mean in 2021 and 2022, altogether, I made almost $4 million in commissions, and I paid only about $250,000 total in taxes. So, that just goes to show how powerful real estate is. If I didn't own real estate, I'd be paying the IRS probably over $1.5 million in taxes. So, think about that; $1.5 million versus $250,000. What kind of position would you rather be in when you have to file taxes and pay the tax man?

That's why it's so important to understand you can't do one without the other. You can't buy real estate if you have no money. Well…you can, but it'll take a lot of your time.

Next let's explore how you can really start making a ton of money, saving up cash, and scaling, and also what not to do.

Chapter Four

STOP WASTING YOUR MONEY!

The thing about money is that it's not about how much you make; it's about how much you save. Most people in the United States lack knowledge of how to save money and how to increase their yearly income. This equation is what helps individuals to break out of the cycle, making it crucial that you understand it to get out of the system.

I've witnessed a lot of horror stories where people start making a lot of money and all their expenses start going up. You may know these kinds of people (or you might have first-hand experience—and no shame if you do). What I mean is, they have that one six-figure year and buy a new BMW or rent that nice apartment downtown on the twenty-second floor that costs double their previous rent. They'll start eating out more. They'll get tables out at the club and get bottle service to impress their peers. They had one stellar year of income and try to act like they're extremely rich when it's actually the opposite.

While it's terrific they are making money, they must save some if they want to break out of the system, work on their own terms, and obtain wealth. In the example I just gave, they're literally spending their money until they become poor. Remember, it's about how much you save, not how much you make. If you make a million dollars a year, but it costs you $900,000 a year to live because you're spending your money on stupid things, your net income is only $100,000. If someone's making $150,000 and living off $40,000, that person had a better year than you financially.

You have to understand that you have to live below your means for a long time and not save all that cash. You read that right, you don't want to save all the cash you have access to. Of course, you want to save some in the bank for a rainy day, but you should strive to save money in the bank only to deploy it into investments or into your own personal development as fast as possible. The bank is where cash goes to die. If your only strategy for wealth is to keep cash in the bank, inflation will slowly eat away your savings, and you'll be less rich if you only keep your money in the bank. This is where many people get this part of the equation wrong.

To get the most out of your money, you should invest it as soon as possible. However, before discussing how to go about investing—which will be covered later on in this book—let's discuss some great ways to save money. This is something that many students won't learn from their teachers and professors in school. The people in the school systems don't want you to know this stuff (or they may not understand it themselves).

If you want to save money, invest in a trustworthy car. Japanese models like Toyota or Honda are excellent choices; they'll run for ages with low maintenance costs compared to other brands. My own experience proves it—I had a Hyundai and drove a Ford Focus through college and the first three years of my real estate career, then passed the Hyundai back to my parents. Yes, I was rolling around in a 2017 Ford Focus to meetings and had a net worth of over a million dollars. That just goes to show that I could live very below my means and quietly and safely grow my investments while not growing my liabilities. I will admit, once I had enough monthly cash flow (passive income) from my investment properties to cover all of my basic living expenses, I did go out and treat myself to nice Mercedes.

So, my second suggestion would be to ensure your cost of living is low. The expensive car and the high rent/mortgage will kill you. Whether you're renting or buying a place, keep your liabilities as low as possible. An effective way to do this is to purchase a duplex, triplex, or fourplex with an FHA loan and rent out the units and your extra bedrooms to tenants. The other tenants paying you rent each month will offset your monthly mortgage payments.

For example, if you purchase a duplex in San Diego and your mortgage payment totals $6,000 per month, consider renting out the other unit for $2,500 a month. This way, instead of paying an entire $6,000 to the bank each month, you can settle with a net of $3,500 without including other minor expenses. Investing in this strategy could be great for those looking to save money when buying a home.

But my advice is to never buy a primary home before you buy an investment property. If you want to buy where you live like I mentioned above, you should always buy a multifamily property. This concept is known as "house hacking."

Recently, a client of mine purchased a fourplex in San Diego for $1.6 million and took out a loan of $1.3 million. The monthly mortgage payment and property taxes came out to around $15,000. He decided to Airbnb the other three units, each of which brought in about $6,000 in income monthly, for a total of $18,000. After all expenses are accounted for (water, sewer, electricity, maintenance), this means that he nets about $1,500 each month from the property.

That's a great way to save and invest and also keep your expenses super low because that same client of mine, he has no living expenses. He doesn't pay rent; he doesn't pay the mortgage. His Airbnb clients are paying the mortgage for him. Think about how much money he's saving in the background while he's still working at his day job. He's a tech sales guy who works for Microsoft, and he's making great money there. Now he's got a side hustle where he is making money from his Airbnb and he gets to live for free. That's my definition of banking cash.

My client is aware of how to stretch his dollars and how integral it is to live beneath one's means in order to acquire more assets. Though he is not financially independent yet, since he still works his job, if he purchases at least one or two properties annually, then he will be on the fast track to financial freedom. This is quite achievable with his wages and controlled spending. Within three to four years, this client will probably be financially free if he stays on the path that he's on right now, and then he can quit his job at Microsoft and live off the cash flow. Using this strategy is great if you're looking to buy where you live.

If you want to break free from the system, I would a hundred percent recommend house hacking or trying to live as close to rent free as possible. If you have the luxury of being able to live with your family, then swallow your ego and do it for a few years while you get your feet moving!

I think the way to keep your rent down as much as possible if you're first getting started, especially if you live in an expensive city like San Diego, is to definitely bunk with your friends. Live with your friends and keep that cost low. My friend lives in an amazing location in San Diego, one of the most expensive cities in America, and he's paying $1,200 a month for a sick room right by the beach. He surfs every morning and lives a great life. All because he uses this same strategy.

You can definitely save money no matter what city you're in. I don't care if you're in Los Angeles, San Francisco, San Diego, or New York. If you can get the right roommates who help support you, who aren't bad influences on you, and who help pay rent so your living costs (your most expensive cost) stay down, then you can bank cash and save as much as possible. Living frugally will get you the opportunity to invest quicker.

If you have managed to accumulate a good sum of savings by living with roommates and diligently applying yourself at your W2 job or business, the worst decision you can make is to spend it all on a primary residence rather than investing in a property.

Think about this. Let's say you are in New York City paying $1,500 a month, and you worked your ass off on Wall Street. You've saved up a good chunk of change. You've saved up $250,000. But you've been given this false image of the

American dream. Your parents and the system say, "Oh, it's time to buy a house. You've saved enough money. Go buy a condo in New York City. It's the AmErIcAn DrEaM!"

If you purchase a condominium for $1 million in New York City rather than investing that money elsewhere, you've essentially given away all of your cash. Yes, it may appreciate in value over time, but instead of paying a mere $1,500 per month to live with friends, you now have a mortgage of $750,000.

And with the current interest rates, your mortgage payment is going to be $8,000 to $9,000 a month, and that's not including property taxes, maintenance, and insurance. Let's just call it $10,000 a month to be safe. You just took your $1,500 a month in living costs, and you basically made it seven times what it was costing you to live in New York City. That is why so many people stay in the middle class. The worst way to use your money is to be multiplying your expenses like that.

I have a client that I just started working with who is kicking themselves for not learning this concept sooner. He is a very hard-working person, and he makes a lot of money as an engineer. His wife is a school teacher. He and his wife, not knowing any better, grinded their tails off and saved money for ten years to buy their dream home here in a nice part of San Diego.

Turns out, before they bought that house, their rent was $3,500 a month for a three-bedroom house in a decent part of town—very manageable for middle- to high-income earners. Guess how much their monthly housing expenses were when they bought their "dream home"?

They were $13,450 a month….

They also were unaware of the unexpected expenses you face when you buy a house that you have to pay as the homeowner.

This includes property taxes, insurance, maintenance costs, landscaping, HOA, and more.

When something breaks in a rental, all you have to do is call your landlord! When something breaks in a house you own, you have to pay for it yourself. To make matters worse, this couple spent 70 percent of their savings on this property. They put down $300,000 to buy this house....

Now, let's say those same people didn't listen to the typical American dream, and they read this book or listened to the right people on the internet. They understand that if they take this $250,000 and put it into an investment property, a four-unit property, or a syndication, whatever it is, they can make at least $1,000 a month in cash flow from that investment and that property will go up in value. They'll be paying down the mortgage because their tenants will be paying down the mortgage for them. Those people, in five to ten years, will be in a much better place financially than the person who bought that condo in New York City.

And keep in mind, rents keep going up and up and up. If you're part of the system now and renting, you know this.

It doesn't matter where you are. Rents will always go up because rents follow inflation. In five to ten years, those people who bought that fourplex with that $250,000 will probably be making somewhere in between $4,000 to $6,000 a month in passive cash flow from that same property (depending on what location they bought in).

While this all sounds incredible, I have to be real with you. A couple of bad decisions can really ruin your investing career. When your investing career is ruined and you can't make enough money to catch up, you're pushing the dream of becoming financially free five to ten years further away. Maybe you were twenty-five years old when you bought that first property and it was a house, and now it might take you until you're forty-five or fifty to be financially free. Had you purchased that fourplex when you bought your first property in your twenties, you would probably have achieved financial independence by the time you turned thirty to thirty-five. This emphasizes that time is the most important asset you have in your life. A few key decisions can make or break your success as an investor. That same couple I mentioned earlier couldn't even think about investing for another ten years out because their monthly expenses were extremely high and their wages didn't keep up.

One of the best ways to save money, particularly in young adulthood, is to reduce how much you go out and limit alcohol consumption. If you're still smoking weed or doing other recreational drugs, it's time to stop. It's a complete waste of money and has no benefit; it's actually decreasing your productivity, harming your physical health, and shortening your lifespan. Drinking and partying multiple nights a week or smoking weed every night will make it very hard to become financially independent.

Not only do those habits kill your nervous system, brain functions, creativity, productivity, and health, it also destroys your bank account.

Purchasing three to five drinks at the bar every night can set someone back around fifty to a hundred dollars. With the addition of a nice dinner, spending easily jumps up to an extra hundred dollars. They buy marijuana from the dispensary once a week, and that costs a couple hundred bucks a week. When adding up all these nights out, it equates to between three hundred to six hundred dollars per week. Taking this figure over fifty weeks leaves one with an eye-opening amount of wasted money; that's $30,000! If individuals are spending this much on alcohol and drugs every week, they could have used it toward their first property instead.

I have a friend who owns a property management company, and he was telling me the other day that he has this employee in his office who makes over six figures a year, but spends it all on food and drinks on the weekends.

He said that his employee gets all of his joy from taking his friends out to eat and he just gorges out on every expensive food item on the menu. Spends an average of $1,000 a night on dinner… The dude spends his entire paycheck on dinners and rent, living paycheck to paycheck.

I mean, wow…. Do what makes you happy, but living paycheck to paycheck and saving zero money would not make me happy. Everyone's different, so I am not going to hate, but that's a sure fire way to never obtain freedom.

The decisions you make every single day in your week, during your month, it can really also make or break your investing career and your chance of being financially free. It's those small decisions that lead you to be healthy, live a good life, have good mental health, and break out of the system.

I understand it's not realistic for me to say never drink alcohol again, but I'm telling you right now, you can save a lot of money on food and alcohol.

When you're young, there are only a few things that really require money: your car, your rent, groceries, and perhaps some recreational spending. If you can be frugal and exercise extreme self-control in these areas, you will free yourself from future financial constraints. To save on groceries and alcohol costs, purchase them in bulk once a week. Go to Costco or Trader Joe's to get the best deals. Additionally, try to meal prep every day to make sure you don't overspend on food. Soon enough, you'll see your savings add up.

I have agents in my office that spend just $200 to $300 per month on food. My favorite example is Sean, who used to come in every week with a rotisserie chicken from Costco. The chicken costs five bucks—plus, he buys pre-cooked rice for about fifty cents each, as well as some vegetables. So, for five days' worth of lunch, this guy only spends around thirty to forty dollars a week.

That's an amazing way to save money while still eating healthy. It was not like he ate ramen and white bread every day.

The way to really save your money to funnel it into investment properties sooner is to limit all these things that can go crazy and eat up your money. If someone gets a really good job, makes six figures a year, there's a serious risk his or her ego will become massive. They'll fall into the traps we talked about. They buy the nice house and the luxury car; they go out to fancy dinners at least twice a week. And at that point, it's going to become impossible to save enough money to be financially free. You have to make good money for three to five years and live like you're broke and invest everything you have left over.

If you really take this to heart, in five to ten years you will be cash flowing so much money, and I promise it's worth the discipline right now. You'll have a great portfolio and you will be a full-time real estate investor in no time by following this plan.

Now, let's talk about how to scale your income. I talked about how to save, but let's talk about the fun stuff. When I say scale it, I mean how to scale your income to where no one else can control it.

Stashing away money is a very crucial habit, but this won't get you to financial freedom if your yearly salary is between

$30,000 to $40,000. Saving doesn't do much good until you increase your income and become a high earner. And with the help of this book, anyone can reach that level.

It doesn't matter what walk of life you're from; it doesn't matter how poor of a family you're from. As you read earlier, I came from a lower to middle class family. My parents combined made like $50,000 to $60,000 a year in California, and my parents both worked overtime to get us out of debt. I say this because anyone reading this can become financially free no matter what situation you are in right now. It doesn't matter who you are, and anyone reading this can make a ton of money.

The fastest way for making the most money while keeping stress and headache to a minimum is to become some kind of salesperson. It's what I did and it worked out well. It doesn't require great skill to start, and anyone can learn how to sell.

I love sales because no one can control how much you make. You're only betting on yourself, and the more you work, the more money you'll bring in, the more commissions you'll make. Becoming a salesperson in some industry you enjoy will allow you to make an unlimited amount of money.

The beauty of sales is that every type of business needs this department to grow as a company, and oftentimes CEOs place the most importance on sales because it creates revenue for the business. Sales is simply making friends with people and letting people know what you have to offer. If you can do that, you can become rich.

There are some sales careers where your commission is limited, and that's the first question you should ask an employer—"Is there a cap on my commission?" If they say yes, walk out of the room and don't look back. As you might already know, my favorite industry for sales is investment real estate.

———

If you are a real estate professional, including residential, commercial, or mortgage brokers, your earnings potential is endless. Your success is limited only by the amount of effort and time you're willing to invest.

I was working sixty to seventy hours a week when I first started banging the phones, networking with people, and trying to call any property owner to see if they'd list their property with me. From reading my story you already know it took me two to three years to become established. And my first year, I barely made any money at all.

In the beginning, when I started out in 2018, nothing came of it and I didn't make any money. But, then in 2019, I made my first $150,000 in commissions, and in 2020, I made $600,000. In 2021, I netted over $1.5 million, and in 2022, I made close to $2 million in commissions. I hate bragging and would never say to this someone out in public, but I only mention my earned income the past few years to show you what is possible. You have to start thinking bigger for yourself!

There are salespeople in every industry. Find any industry that you love. It can be music, any sort of art, computers, technology, or medical sales. You can be in printer sales if you're passionate about printers; you can be in laptop sales; you can be in landscaping sales; you can be in construction sales. It doesn't matter. There's so many different industries out there where sales people are critical and absolutely necessary.

If you are looking to become financially free, you have to learn how to sell. The most successful entrepreneurs in the world know how to sell. Mark Cuban, Jeff Bezos, and Elon Musk all have an exceptional ability to sell and pitch their ideas and products.

I have a few friends in tech sales who make multiple six figures a year by simply sending out emails and not having to get on the phone very often. There is potential to craft an entire sales career without relying on face-to-face conversations or verbal communication, if that's what you'd prefer. By writing emails, messaging people through apps, and having perhaps a couple of Zoom meetings, it's all doable.

No matter what your skill set is, anyone can become a good salesperson. All it takes is communication. And as humans, we were born to communicate with others. If we're born to communicate, that means anyone can become a salesperson.

The other best strategy, of course, as you probably know, is to become an entrepreneur. This is a lot more work, but some people can take it because they want to have their own brand like I did. They want to have their own company, and they want to be their own boss.

All in all, it could be quite amazing when you are passionate about what you do. The factor that will make or break you as an entrepreneur is how much pleasure you get from your work.

If you hate what you do every single day and you're just in it for the money, you're not going to have any passion. You're going to get burned out. You're going to fail. The people who love what they do and who you hate, they're going to crush you in that industry because they can work a lot more hours while actually enjoying what they do. Find what you love and just pick one thing. Don't jump around from industry to industry. The grass is not greener on the other side. The grass is greener where you water it.

When I first started as an entrepreneur, I had the same issue. I thought about maybe selling digital products, being an e-commerce guru, selling products on Amazon, marketing, or starting a social media marketing agency. I thought all these ways were great ways to make money. I jumped to literally every single one of those.

It was only when I got into real estate because I had a passion for it that I stopped changing paths frequently. I hadn't cared for any of the other careers, and so I kept hopping from one place to another, going nowhere.

When I jumped to the real estate game, I really made headway and actually made legitimate progress.

I am biased here, but being a multifamily real estate agent is the fastest and most simple way to become wealthy while you're young. I have several acquaintances and friends in this business in their late twenties and early thirties who are making well over $1 million a year doing what I do.

Some of my agents are in their early twenties making multiple six figures a year, and they are getting ready to buy their first investment property in less than a year. That's so powerful. When you can start compounding in your early twenties, there is a 100 percent chance you will become a multimillionaire.

How many multimillionaires do you know in their mid-twenties?

If you want to be a part of the case study and are interested in making over $1 million a year, I personally train and coach ten agents per year. You know where to find me if you think you are a good fit.

You are an entrepreneur and a sales person when you are an agent. It's the best business in the world.

Don't make the same mistakes I made. Don't make the same mistakes other people I know have made. Save as much money as possible when you're young, and live like you're broke. I don't care how much money you're making—live like you're broke and live humbly. Don't let anyone know you're making a lot of money; just know that you're on the journey to financial freedom. In your heart, you know that time freedom, financial freedom, and not having to hit the clock every morning at 9:00 a.m. is the most important value you have. You have to sacrifice a lot of other things in order to get to that place. Then you can do all the things you want to do.

When motivation starts to slip, remind yourself that financial freedom will grant you the opportunity to visit any place you desire. Paris, Tokyo, anywhere in the United States, or beyond—if it's out there, you can make it happen. You have all the time in the world!

You will be able to book a trip from Monday to Friday without having to report to a boss and without asking for PTO. You can hang out with your family and your kids without having to ask for permission. You can do whatever you want, and that's why it's so important to start banking cash and then investing it.

In order to reach financial freedom, you must become a high-earning individual, be it as a real estate agent, marketer, or business owner—something that provides you with an income that's not subject to external control. Save and invest all the money you make into cash flowing assets and watch your wealth grow over time until you are financially free with your entire life ahead of you.

Chapter Five

HOW TO KNOW YOU'RE READY TO START INVESTING

There's really no magic number for knowing if you are ready to invest. It's something that lives within yourself and your desires. So remember what we talked about assessing your financials (your monthly expenses and income), what your bank account looks like, and what your current investments are (if you have any). Then ask yourself, "Am I ready to put money to work?" That answer should come as soon as possible. If you're comfortable with your financial situation, you have to start in real estate right away.

One rule that my CPA and other very intelligent real estate investors taught me is that you need six months of savings in your bank account. This rule allows you to be conservative for emergencies but still invest. After six months of savings are in the bank, then invest everything else. What are your living expenses for six months? If your rent is $2,000, food is $1,000, car payment is $1,000, and other miscellaneous stuff is $1,000, then your living costs are $5,000 a month. You should have $5,000 times six, or $30,000, in the bank in case of an emergency because you still have that income coming in. So no matter what, your bank accounts keep growing. Hopefully, you're making over five grand a month, so you're constantly saving a lot of money each month.

Let's say now you have that $30,000 in the bank for emergencies. You reach $60,000 in the bank by using the strategies we discussed. If you have $60,000 in the bank, then $30,000 should go to a real estate investment. Whether it's a syndication or a partnership, whatever it is, put that money to work. The remaining $30,000 is your emergency fund and should stay in the bank. However, $30,000 isn't enough to invest on your own—but more on that later.

When you invest your money for the first time, it's normal to feel scared and anxious. I was very nervous when I made my first investment, more nervous than most people. I couldn't sleep at night because I worried about losing all my money, and my stomach was always upset. That's how humans are: uneasy with new things and with leaving our comfort zone. Investing in the right assets can cause discomfort, but it's a good sign of growth and financial security.

If you find yourself feeling a bit out of your comfort zone, a bit scared or nervous, it means you're making progress. You are taking strides toward achieving financial freedom. If you feel stressed and negative, it means you're on the path to your dream life. All will be well. You are growing.

I did not know what I was getting into when I first began a real estate internship that paid zero in salary, only commissions. Within me, though, I knew that this would get me closer to where I wanted to go. When I bought my first investment property, I was nervous about all the potential mistakes I might make. But, in my gut, I knew this was how I could achieve my main goal: giving back to my family and achieving financial freedom for us. I felt nervous when I started my own business after leaving my old real estate company. Because I was scared and apprehensive, experiencing a mix of emotions, I asked many people for advice. I did it anyway because I knew it would help me achieve my goals. My goal was to create a company filled with people I loved working with where I could help everyone win as a team. My core values and goals were leading me down this path, so I stuck to it.

So I know it can be scary, but when you have that positive feeling in your gut, it means one thing: you're ready.

If you've used the strategies from this book so far, you're well on your way. Your bank account is growing, you're spending less than you earn, and you know that investing a little money can be better than working harder. Remember that money never sleeps, so it's only working for you. It works full time, twenty-four hours a day, seven days a week, all the time. It's always working for you. It's always growing for you (if invested correctly).

I don't know about you, but I can't work twenty-four hours a day, seven days a week. So the more money you put into investing, the harder it's going to work for you. If you have the savings but you haven't invested, remember, time is not on your side. Start as soon as possible. Life is short. The people who give bad advice will always tell you, "Time is on your side. You have all the time in the world. Take your time." No, that's bullshit. You want to start as soon as possible and get into it as fast as you can because the longer you're in the real estate game, the richer you're going to be and the sooner you are going to have the freedom you have dreamed of.

Now, let's focus on understanding your goals, who you are, and how you wish to invest. This is crucial because my objectives differ from yours. Everyone reading this book has different goals. To succeed, you need to understand yourself, your goals, and what you want to achieve in the next five to ten years. Have a plan in mind that will lead you closer to your aspirations. You need some plan of action or else it won't happen. You must take steps to meet your ambitions.

I encourage you to really assess yourself. Put the book down and think about it for five to ten minutes, ideally in your journal. In five years, where do you want to be? How much money do you want to make a year in passive cash flow? How do you want to be spending the majority of your time? What do you want your core values to be? What do you want your day-to-day to look like? How do you want to feel? How do you want to be thinking? Who do you want surrounding you? You have to take all these things into account.

And here's the thing: the bigger your goals are, the more you're going to have to sacrifice. Let's say there's person A and person B. Person A, let's call Joe. Joe is someone who's simple. He wants to earn $80,000 a year without working, and he wants to travel with his wife. He also wants to spend more time outdoors, hiking and doing what he enjoys, rather than being stuck at a desk job. Let's look at person B. Person B is Sean. Sean wants to make $1 million a year passively and also run a successful business making $10 million annually. He wants to have a wife and three kids. He wants to spend a lot of time going to different countries.

Joe and Sean will have completely different paths in life. Sean will need to give up more, work longer hours, and likely have less time for other relationships than Joe. Joe can relax, go at a slower pace, enjoy the journey, and reduce stress. He won't have as much to do. If you want to make a million a year in passive income like Sean versus $80,000 like Joe, you might need to own fifty to one hundred properties depending on the location. Joe might only have to own three. So right away you can see that those are two totally different paths.

Maybe some of you want to be Sean, and maybe some of you just want to be Joe. That's why you really have to understand who you are and how you want to invest. Because if you don't understand what kind of life you want to build, you'll be running toward nothing and you're going to get burned out. So you have to have some plan in mind because real estate is not the end goal. Real estate is not the pot of gold at the end of the rainbow. It's really not. Real estate's a vehicle; it's a tool to help you do what you want to do with your life.

I know that for most of you reading this book, real estate is not going to be your number one passion. It's just not true for most people. The fastest and easiest way to free up your time is to create passive income. With more time, you can focus on your passions, like family or hobbies. You can also pursue speaking gigs, music, charity, or anything you've always wanted to do. Imagine having seven days a week to pursue that instead of having to worry about a nine to five. That's why real estate is amazing. It helps you build the life you want.

I'm not saying it's not going to take sacrifice, it's not going to take longer hours, and it's not going to take you having to maybe skip Friday and Saturday nights with your friends.

If you're thirty years old and not anywhere close to financial freedom, the key is a new sales career or a business where only you can control your income. Work hard and bring in six figures annually while living off only $3,000 monthly by maybe sharing a place with roommates and not going out to eat much. Do this for three to four years while investing in one property each year, and you'll soon be on your way to being financially free. Take it further for five to seven years and by the time you're thirty-seven or thirty-eight, you will have some significant cash flow. That's the power of real estate.

One of my clients has an amazing story. He was broke until he was thirty-five years old, working at a tire mechanic shop in a rough part of San Diego. He lived paycheck to paycheck, and he and his wife fought about money constantly. They couldn't support their family of four with their current income, and they could never save up enough money to get ahead.

Then one day, he had a breaking point. He had enough. He applied for over fifty jobs and finally landed a job selling printers. All he had to do was make phone calls and sell printers to businesses. After doing manual labor for almost twenty years, he thought sitting at a desk and talking to people was the easiest job in the world.

He ended up making over $500,000 a year after a few years in that business and started accumulating small investment properties around town. Every single year, he would save up to buy at least one investment property.

He is now worth over $30 million at age fifty and is a retired, "full-time" real estate investor.

Worrying about money is my biggest nightmare. It's something I never want to do ever again because I dealt with it growing up. I saw my parents fight and watched them struggle. So that trauma is a wall that I want to run as far away from as I can, and that's what real estate has done for me. So let that passive income, that cash flow, build a life that you want to live. And it starts with making that first investment, maybe even going into it full time.

If you have a passion for the game, then real estate can be incredibly rewarding. If you're someone who enjoys the hustle, it's possible to make it as a full-time investor, agent, lender, or property manager. Starting your own real estate business and running an investment venture on the side is an amazing way to build your empire even faster. This could help you become the next Sean, one of the most successful individuals in the world of real estate. Whether you're Joe or Sean, real estate offers enormous potential for building a diverse portfolio, creating the life you want, and achieving financial freedom.

Chapter Six

YOUR FIRST 25K: GETTING INVOLVED IN SYNDICATIONS

The definition of syndication and how it can benefit you when you first start is simple. A syndication, in the simplest terms, is when a general partner (the main buyer) pools money from many different investors (limited partners) and invests the funds to buy a property. Typically, you'll see syndicators buy a development deal, apartment complex, retail center, or something along those lines. They can buy whatever real estate asset they want; it's just a way to pool money and combine funds to buy a property. When you first get started in real estate investing, partnering in a syndication is a great strategy to get your feet wet.

There are rules of a syndication, but to save you the time, the main rule you should know is that your money is committed to the property for as long as the general partner (or the person who runs the deal and makes all the decisions) wants to sell or refinance to pay back your capital.

In real estate syndication, you need to look at the long-term: investments can take anywhere from two to ten years to see a return on. Be prepared to commit your money for the duration. When you're starting out, you likely won't have much experience or cash—usually you need at least $20,000 to $25,000 to get involved. This is why investing in a syndication is so powerful because saving up $100,000 to $400,000 is much harder than $25,000 when it comes to investing in your first property. On top of that, great general partners will give you a higher return than the property you would go out on your own to buy.

Many syndicators have a minimum of $50,000, but you can find some great ones for $25,000. Once that's saved up, however, you'll gain access to a range of opportunities. The most important factor in any deal is the general partner, so choose wisely. The operator is more important than the deal.

You'll want to make sure that the person you invest with is someone who's experienced, knows their market, has a track record of getting amazing returns for their investors, does a good job, communicates well, and, most importantly, is just a good person overall who's going to do the right thing.

Investing in a syndication when you first get started in the real estate world means you can learn from much more experienced people who are also invested in that deal. There's usually two to five general partners that manage the deal, and if you invest in one of their properties, you have access to those people.

When you speak with the investor, you can ask them any questions about the investment or the business plan. Find out what they think makes it a good opportunity, what risks there might be, and the pros and cons of investing in it. Do your due diligence by getting as much information from the investor as possible before making a decision.

Having access to their knowledge and getting these insights allows you to learn very quickly and fast track your success. Meanwhile, you're passively investing without it taking up any of your time because the general partners are doing all the work. As a limited partner, all you have to do is invest your money and that money will go to work for you. On average, you want a 15 percent to 20 percent return a year. They call it IRR, internal rate of return. This basically means if you put in $100,000, you better expect to make, to accrue equity and cash flow, a total of at least $15,000 to $20,000 a year. You can see already that this is much better than investing in the stock market since the market only returns an average of 8 percent per year.

So in order to have your money tied up, because that's the con of being in a syndication, you want to make sure that you're getting a really good return. So if you're getting 15 percent to 20 percent returns a year and you're doubling your money in five to seven years, you're doing very well. That's when it's worth it to tie your money up in an investment property. And not only that, you get all the benefits of being a real estate investor. You get appreciation from the property, and you get cash. So, you're building equity, and—my favorite reason to invest in real estate—you're getting tax benefits.

You'll get a tax return document called a K-1 that will most likely show a "negative return" especially in year one. The deal is making money, but it just shows a negative return because of depreciation and cost segregation, which I'll explain in later chapters, but that's the beauty of owning real estate. You can make money, make big returns, but also lower your tax liability, which is the most important part of building wealth, especially if you're a high-income earner.

In California, if you make $150,000 a year, you're only actually netting about $90,000 to $100,000 a year because the IRS and the State of California is taking a huge chunk of your income. So you have to find a way to put your money in a tax advantageous vehicle like real estate, and getting into syndication when you might not have a lot of money—when you're younger or just getting started in your career—is the fastest way to learn and to get into the game of real estate.

So those are the main benefits. You can learn from people who are much more experienced than you. You get all the benefits of owning real estate, you don't need a lot of money to start, and, most importantly, you're a passive investor. You're not an active investor.

It's essential to grasp the contrast between active and passive investing.

When you're an active investor, real estate takes time out of your week. You are building a business when you are buying properties, but if you're investing in syndications, it's purely investing and doesn't take up any of your time (just like stocks). It's a great way to start your journey, and you can stay in syndications your whole life if you never want to manage real estate. I know many people who only invest passively and who have very successful businesses. They don't want to waste any more of their time because time is the most valuable asset you have. They can make money in their business and not spend extra time growing and managing a real estate portfolio. Passive investing works really well for people who are making a lot of money in other careers or other businesses.

So let's get into what all you need to start. The reason why the $25,000 is the magic number is because for 99 percent of syndications out there, the minimum is $25,000. Of course, there are syndications where the minimum is higher, more like $50,000 to $100,000, but you can find a lot of great deals for a $25,000 minimum.

If you can't come up with the $25,000 needed for a real estate investment, then it's time to go back and review chapters one through five of your plan. Work to increase your income so that you have more money saved.

I know a lot of gurus out there tell you you can get started in real estate with little to no money, but you need at least $25,000 to get started. That's not a lot of money. If you think it is, you have to change your mindset about money.

Now, let's get into the nitty-gritty of how to find great operators and what qualities you should look for.

When you search for an operator, it must be somebody who has a thorough knowledge of your market—regardless of whether that may be in California, Florida, Arizona, or elsewhere. You should make sure they have already invested in properties within the area.

If they don't have properties there and they're entering a market for the first time, I'd highly recommend steering away from that syndication because chances are there's a lot of mistakes that the sponsor or the general partner is going to make. Next, before investing heavily, you need to make sure that they have a high experience level. If you approach a syndication and they only have one or two properties under their belt, I'd highly recommend running away in the other direction. Let other people invest in that syndication and take that risk.

To be sure of their skills, ask potential investors to show you at least ten to successful properties in their portfolio. These investments should showcase how they purchased a property, followed through with the business plan—whether it was renovation or development—and either resold the asset or refinanced it for a much higher value, giving their financiers the return they anticipated.

Don't shy away from asking about the syndication's successful exits. I look for at least five to seven successful exits before I even consider a syndication. You want to make sure they've seen a deal from start to finish multiple times.

When vetting a great operator, you want to make sure that they're giving you fair returns. So in a typical syndication, there's what's called a preferred return. A preferred return is the accrued, or sometimes simple, interest. It's the interest that the limited partner gets before the general partner makes any money. So what a standard simple syndication looks like is I'll give the investor an 8 percent preferred return per year. If you put in $100,000, you're going to make $8,000 a year.

Then after that 8 percent is satisfied, the general partner gets a "promote." In simplest terms, the promote is the profit that the general partner receives for managing the investment and satisfying the preferred return. After the 8 percent preferred return is hit, the limited partners (LPs) receive a 70 percent profit split of the deal proceeds. Typically, a general partner will not see any of these profits until a big capital event occurs, such as a cash-out refinance or a sale of the property.

Now, if that 8 percent is not hit in year one or two because of major renovations or other things, we make sure that the 8 percent accrues compound interest into the next year (and it'll go up and up) if we don't meet that 8 percent threshold. This allows for our investors to get maximum returns. Typically, by the time they get the 8 percent return and the 70 percent profits, our returns have been anywhere from 15 percent to 25 percent. On one deal we just flipped, we had a 35 percent IRR and all our investors were extremely happy. In that instance, one investor put in $100,000, and six months later, they got $35,000 in profits. So not a bad deal at all, and they did nothing as well. Where else can you find those sort of returns?

If an operator is only giving you a 5 percent preferred return and they're getting most of the profits, you should highly reconsider what you're looking at. Let's say you're still making a 20 percent return; maybe that's an okay deal. But if the general partner is making more of a percentage than the limited partners, then I'd highly recommend walking away from that property. It means they're probably greedy and you're not going to get the money you want out of the deal. Never partner with someone who takes more than a 50 percent promote.

A lot of general partners (GPs) structure their promote in what is a called a "waterfall." People explain in very confusing ways, but I will make it very understandable for you. Let's say you invest in a piece of property in San Diego, and the syndicators you invest with project a 20 percent return year over year with a 30 percent promote in place. In case the deal over performs and does much better, what the GP will do is put in a waterfall. So if the deal returns 25 percent to the LPs, then the promote will be 40 percent to the GP. Once the deal returns 30 percent to LPs, then the promote to the GP will be 50 percent.

This is just an example, and it can be structured in many different ways, so make sure you ask how the deal is structured before you put your hard-earned money into an investment opportunity.

Another aspect you need to make sure you're aware of when looking for a good operator is that they're very transparent.

If they're not straightforward and clear with you about their practices, like hiding the numbers or not revealing how much money is involved or being evasive about what taxes are owed, you should never work with them again.

The way to avoid that is to ask for referrals. Get at least two or three referrals from limited partners and ask them how transparent the general partner is about the numbers and about how the deal operates.

I prefer to keep our clients and partners meticulously informed during all phases of our deals. We provide them with in-depth updates; show the property's current status at all stages of the construction, including its appearance; give updates on the numbers; and supply projections for expected returns.

We are very active in showing our investors how the property is doing because communication is key and I'd much rather over communicate than under communicate.

There are a lot of operators out there, some great and some not so good.

Muddling through the path of finding a good operator can be tough, but LinkedIn is a great resource for locating multi-family syndication networking groups that are a good match. Alternatively, social media platforms such as YouTube or podcasts are also great places to find high-quality operators looking to raise more money. I suggest checking out various real estate channels and seeing what they bring to the table. However, make sure you thoroughly vet them and ask the tough questions before committing to anything.

Another great way to find excellent general partners and syndication operators is to look for people who are already invested in those deals as a passive investor, like myself. I can give you lots of great referrals on who to invest with, but there are a lot of people just like me. You can go to Facebook groups, look up networking groups, and talk to people that are local in your area to find someone. If you're in a big city, there's probably a syndication networking group meeting every single day. So go network, go meet these people. You'll need to find people that are actively doing these kinds of deals and see who they refer to you because referrals are the best possible ways to find great connections.

If you put in $25,000 and you make a 20 percent return a year, that's $5,000 a year. So if you are invested in a property for five years, the general partner, the syndicator, buys the property in year one and sells in year five. If you held that property for five years, you should have doubled your money if you got a 20 percent return each year because $5,000 times five years is $25,000. So if you put in $25,000 or if you put in $100,000, you're going to double your money in five years if you bought into a 20 percent IRR.

Another metric you need to look for is what's called the equity multiple. This shows how much you've multiplied your money and you should see it in every syndicator's underwriting. A 2x equity multiple means you will have doubled your money by the time the property is sold or refinanced. So, if you put in a $100,000 investment and you got a 3.02x equity multiple in five years, that means you now have $302,000. You turned your $100,000 into $302,000, which basically means you tripled your money, and that is an amazing investment for not doing any work or spending any time out of your day to make sure the investment was doing well.

For these reasons, real estate syndication is truly one of the best investments out there and the least risky if you're partnering with good people. When you are starting out with little money and still trying to learn the game, this is the best way to go.

Everything we've discussed so far is for passive investing. I want to switch it up and talk about active investing in real estate. If you're fired up about the ideas in this book and looking to be an active investor, I want to tell you the pros and cons of both active and passive so you have all the information.

As an active investor, you're buying your own property, financing the property, finding properties, talking to brokers, executing the remodel, and managing the construction. You're going to be managing the property, whether it's you or your property manager, and doing the accounting and taxes and all the things that require operating a property. That's why it's called being an active investor, because it's not passive. You're actively doing things that take time out of your day.

Joining a syndication is truly passive, while active investing takes time out of your schedule. But the pros of being an active investor is you get to call the shots. You're more liquid because you choose when you want to sell or when you don't want to sell. You have all the authority to make decisions on the property and, if you don't have any partners, you are the sole decision maker. You can do whatever you want and you get all the cash flow; you get all the tax benefits and all the appreciation. So you get a bigger piece of the pie (or the entire pie), but you're doing more work, and it takes more time to do that.

There are pros and cons of being a passive investor too. The pros are easy to see—you're not doing any work. You're getting all the benefits of owning real estate without spending a second out of your day besides wiring your money to the syndicator, and you're seeing all the things that happen in a deal.

One con, of course, is that you're paying the syndicator fees, so you're giving up some of the profits to the syndicator. So not all the money you make is yours. You need to be very cognizant of what fees the syndicator is charging because they'll charge a 1 percent to 2 percent acquisition fee, which is the fee a syndicator charges when they acquire a property. For example, if a syndicator raises money and buys a 1 million dollar property, then the syndicator will take a fee of $10,000 from the investors.

They'll charge a 1 to 5 percent asset management fee and possibly other fees. Make sure you're not dealing with a syndicator that's just charging a bunch of fees and you're dealing with a fair and honest group. Some of those fees are fair because they're spending time out of their week to actively manage your money and actively increase your income in your investment.

It's like consulting a financial adviser. They're taking a commission and paid to manage your finances for you, so you don't have to lift a finger. The main factor to consider with syndication is what kind of return you'll get on your investment. Regardless of the fees the syndicator charges, if you see 15 to 20 percent returns every year, then it's a great deal and you have nothing to complain about.

If you're interested in one of our syndications, feel free to email me. My email is jason@jlmcre.com. We have new properties available most of the time, so if you have interest in partnering with us and learning from us, feel free to contact me.

Chapter Seven

THE RIGHT PARTNERS WILL MAKE YOU WEALTHIER

Before you get anxious from this chapter, let me first say the $100,000 is not a set in stone number. It's just a threshold to show you that you'll need a little more money and knowledge, a little more experience under your belt, if you want to come into the partnership world. In the last chapter, we discussed just getting involved with syndications. In those scenarios, you were just a limited partner. You didn't have any say in the deal. You didn't have any control in the deal. You were just, what I call, a silent partner, someone who's along for the ride.

If you want to become an experienced real estate investor, you need to be the one taking control, making decisions, and be a part of the executive team, rather than just being a limited or silent partner. However, if that's not something you want to do—whether it's because you don't have the time or the drive—there's nothing wrong with being a limited partner in a syndication. If your career is very time-consuming but comes with a lot of money, like a doctor or lawyer, it may be beneficial to stay there until you have more free time.

But, even if you don't plan on actively owning real estate, I still think it's beneficial to finish reading this book. It will help you understand how the operators or general partners, who actually own and manage the assets, think. So, even for pure educational purposes, these chapters are very important.

In the case you aspire to advance from a 30 percent owner to a 100 percent owner, you must keep reading.

From my observations and experience with the individuals I've worked with and from the wealthy investors I've been lucky to call my clients, all of them are majority owners in their investments. They have huge stakes in all their properties; some own a whopping five thousand units without having any partners at all. It's simply incredible.

Rapid expansion and ultimately becoming a sole owner of your real estate portfolio is the best outcome one can hope for. No partners, no boss above you—complete freedom. That is the goal when it comes to owning property.

You make all the decisions. You don't spend any time on your properties because you have a team that spends their time running it for you. So I think that's the holy grail of owning real estate. That's how all my biggest clients operate at this point in their lives because they've been doing it for thirty, forty, or fifty years.

Forming a partnership is the way to take your real estate venture to the next level. When you enter into a joint venture, your name is in the LLC operating agreement as a managing member, so you share in the decision making and, of course, a big part of the cash flow. It's an excellent way to make more money together. Hence the arbitrary number of $100,000; it highly depends what market you're in. In San Diego, two or three people with $100,000 each won't give you too many options for multifamily properties, but in the sunbelt or the Midwest, that'll get you a solid number of multifamily units.

That's why there isn't a specific dollar number to reach; but rather, the reason why you're progressing is because you want to move faster. You aim for more cash, increased wealth, and self-development. That is what will take you to the next stage. And this would be that level.

To be a valuable addition to any team, you must bring more than just money. You need to contribute something operationally significant. This could mean having the skills or expertise for finding and acquiring deals, managing the construction phase, or being an excellent asset manager. Alternatively, you might have extensive accounting experience and excel in a CFO type of role. Being able to add value beyond mere cash is truly invaluable in any business.

My partner and I are fifty-fifty in our partnership, and it could not be going better. We scaled our partnership to a net worth of over $8 million in less than three years. I'm skilled in acquisitions and construction management while my partner is an accountant who shines at financial analysis, filing taxes properly, and bookkeeping. Our different skill sets and the value we add to each other have proven to be very successful. We each contribute unique skill sets that make our partnership strong and fast-growing.

He is also much more liquid than I am. He has a much higher net worth. And when someone has a high net worth, this allows them to get better financing. If you bank with any bank in the world, and there's an investor who has $100 million net worth versus a $10 million net worth, I promise you the person with $100 million net worth will be treated much better, get a better interest rate/term sheet, and have a higher likelihood for financing and funding that property.

This is an example of how you have a successful partnership. You want to have a partner or partners where each person brings different things to the table.

If all of you and your partners have the same exact skill sets, such as acquisitions, but none of you have any experience or expertise in property management or construction management, then you won't have a successful team. This is because all of you will be competing for the same tasks and won't be able to handle the other elements of real estate ownership that require specialized knowledge and skills. As a result, there will be disagreements about the direction to take, which can lead to a breakdown in your partnership. So having different skill sets to add to the table is extremely important.

Having different personality types is essential, too. I would recommend you and your potential partners to take a DISC test. This test will allow you to assess your personality types and how you think and act in certain situations.

For example, when you and your partner go to buy a property and you are trying to assess whether or not it is a good investment, it can be detrimental if both of you move extremely fast and make quick decisions. You might miss something critical.

Now, if one partner moves and make decisions very fast, and one partner is more slow and methodical and analyzes everything very deeply, that partner will help the other see any blind spots that they didn't account for.

The two partners who move extremely fast and will invest in something without knowing everything might have purchased a property without realizing the entire sewer line had to be replaced. They weren't thorough enough.

The one analytical partner would have been more thorough in their inspections and would have done a sewer scope to assess the health of the sewer line.

If everyone is super type A, you're probably going to have some head-to-head battles. You're probably going to have some issues, and I've had that in the past. So make sure to have diversity in order to have a successful partnership when it comes to skillset and personality types.

Another key to a successful partnership, or being a good partner, is understanding what you're good at and what you enjoy. Focusing on one or two things that you are the best at doing is important. If you complete tasks that you hate doing, eventually it will harm everyone involved. So, what is your one thing? What is the one thing that you can bring to the table that you love and that you're also really good at? Because that is how you're going to enjoy being a real estate owner and being in business with other people. So, you want to build the skills that you enjoy doing most. You want to lean into that skill set and bring that value, show that value, and keep doing it to show your partners that you are someone who's worth having on the team.

If you're reading this book, chances are you may be the partner with less expertise, as you likely have less experience. My partners in the beginning all had more experience than me. So when you're going to a partnership, especially if you're young and hungry, it's very crucial to be with partners that are more experienced than you. And you want to make sure that for the exchange of knowledge and money that they're bringing to the table, you want to bring in hustle, a little bit of money, and, most importantly, your time.

Wealthier individuals, those who have had multiple businesses and own many pieces of property, view time to be much more valuable than money. As a result, they would rather spend less time handling real estate transactions or anything else related to it. If you are willing to give up your time for the experience, knowledge, and shares in real estate deals, then you will gain more equity from your partners—making it the ideal partnership when starting out. That's how I started. That's how many people before me started.

Not all partnerships are going to go well. I've seen both failed and successful partnerships and I've got some big takeaways for you. One of my most memorable failed partnerships happened just a couple years ago when I had found a seventy-six-unit portfolio in San Diego County. I found it off-market from a friend of mine, and I was trying to find a good loan broker or mortgage broker for the property. I asked a friend who was interested in putting money in if he had any other partners that were also well capitalized that wanted to be a part of the deal.

My friend said to me, "Yes, I know this guy named John." I'm not going to mention his actual name in the book, but I'll refer to him as John. When I met John, we got together for coffee. He was a bit quiet and reserved but he seemed nice. He was much older; he must have been around seventy years old. He was very well-off and a successful real estate developer in San Diego. After I met him the first time, he said that he would consider partnering with us.

But as time went on, our relationship got worse and worse because he really was a control freak. He wanted to be the only boss in this deal. He attempted to control me and tell me what to do. I felt that I had valuable ideas and contributions, but he thought differently. He thought the in-house operation at his company was way more valuable than anything I could bring to the table. And of course, when one of your partners has that mindset, it's a partnership that's going to fail.

I was sitting in his office in San Diego surrounded by his construction team and partners when one of the women asked me, "What do you bring to the table?" I wanted to say nothing, but instead I said, "I found this deal. I'm experienced in acquisitions, construction management, and negotiating deals. So yeah, I have a lot to offer."

She came back with a snappy comment. "Oh, well then if you're doing that, we're going to be working very close together because I'm going to make sure that you don't screw anything up." There was a distinguishable age difference between her and I, so I got the impression she thought I was probably incapable.

As soon as that meeting ended, I knew I couldn't work with those people anymore. They were just too frustrating to deal with, no matter how much money I could potentially make from this property.

So I said, screw that, I'm out of here. John and I ended up splitting ways. I got my initial deposit out of escrow and I said,

"You know what? You could have it. Move on. It's not worth my mental health." So that was that.

I once had another venture that didn't go too well with a partner. He would call me multiple times just to ask silly questions, even though I had far more experience with our project. Despite the irritation he caused me right from the start, I still attempted to remain civil and communicate with him. But the reason why this was a failing partnership and I won't buy another deal with him is because he's very greedy and he's dishonest.

Before making the purchase, we discussed the terms and conditions. Every time I thought we had it all figured out, he changed his story. "We're fifty-fifty" turned into "sixty-forty," which then became "seventy-thirty," and eventually "eighty-twenty." He kept shifting the percentages around with no explanation other than saying, "I thought we talked about this." It was almost like he was trying to manipulate or gaslight me into thinking that I had said something wrong.

I'm not someone who is very confrontational, and I don't enjoy arguing or fighting with people. With him, I said something like, "You know what? It's fine. I have the experience. You have the money." When I bought this deal, I was out of capital. I had no liquidity. So I put in $50,000 and he put in $500,000. So whatever. It's fine. We bought a good deal together. It's working out. We're probably going to sell it or refinance soon. But his character and his personality type doesn't fit with me, and I can't deal with dishonest people. So, of course, it's not going to work out. We still own the property together, but when we sell it, good riddance.

On the flip side, I've had two very successful partnerships who I've bought most of my properties with. With one partner, him and I, we get along very, very well. He doesn't annoy me. He's busy. I'm busy. This is the guy I talked about early in the chapter, how he's the one that manages the finances. I'm more the construction and acquisitions guy. I'm the front end; he's the back end. So it works very well.

My other successful partnership works very much the same way, except the other two partners are more operational, which I like. I just focus my time on acquisitions. They focus kind of more on the operational business side of things. I love acquisitions, so I'm really happy about that.

We've done some really profitable deals together, thanks to our combined skill sets. Moreover, we've been able to raise funds from our friends and family. It's been a true testament to the trust and respect of those close to us.

We bought a property for $1.3 million about six months ago, and we just flipped it for about almost $2.1 million. We invested $200,000 into the venture and generated a major return. Everyone netted over a 100 percent return in just half a year—remarkable.

Those are examples of both successful and unsuccessful collaborations.

My biggest takeaway for you from this chapter is if you are looking to grow and expand your real estate portfolio as fast as possible while gaining a ton of knowledge, make sure to partner with one to three other people and also make sure you have some sort of control in the decision making. Join a partnership where you can learn from people that are much more knowledgeable than you, and you will be a pro in less than a few years.

Surround yourself with the people that you want to become. I know people that have found very, very good mentors and partners through joining coaching groups and masterminds.

But whether it's mine or someone else's, join a group where there are other people that want to do the same thing and have the same mindset as you.

Just like finding syndications, you can find partners by attending meetups around your town. If you're in a big city like San Diego or Los Angeles or Chicago, I promise you there are at least two to three real estate meetups a week in your city. They happen all the time. So go there and network, show your face. Another way to find great partners is to simply be a good business person, whether it's in real estate or something else. I think this is the best way, but you have to find a way to add value to the marketplace and gain a good track record prior to offering or trying to pitch yourself to other investors to partner with.

For example, if you're looking to find partners but you have no business experience, I'd highly recommend becoming a real estate broker or a real estate agent, like I was, and adding value to real estate investors by finding them good deals. I found my best partner by doing about twenty deals with him, repping them on the buy side, and selling some properties for him. Eventually, we built a great relationship. Our relationship formed organically, and we both thought it'd be a great idea to partner with each other for future properties. He knew that I was a hard worker with a great track record. I'd done a lot of deals in real estate as a young hustler and he noticed that about me.

So if you want to find the quickest way to get real estate experience and to really find great partners, become a commercial real estate broker. And if you're interested in learning more about that, feel free to reach out to me via email at jason@jlm-cre.com. We are growing fast and want to partner with young, hardworking people who just need accountability and knowledge to become their best self.

Chapter Eight

OWNING AND CONTROLLING YOUR FIRST MULTIFAMILY PROPERTY

D ue to me going all in as a multifamily real estate agent and selling over thirty properties in 2019 and 2020, I had managed to save up approximately $500,000. That finally gave me the confidence to buy my first property on my own in San Diego. This property that I bought in 2020 still brings me the most cash flow a month to this day.

I own way bigger properties than this property, but it just goes to show that if you are a hundred percent owner of something that's worth $2 million, it's better than being a 5 percent owner of something worth $20 million. At this level, you don't have partners, you don't have anyone telling you what to do with your money. You're not sharing the pot with anyone else. It's just me. And I'm getting all the cash flow, all the profits from the property.

I bought this property for $630,000, and I put $400,000 into it by renovating the two units and then building two ADUs or accessory dwelling units to the lot by converting the garages. My fourplex appraised for $2.1 million after I added the two ADUs and fully renovated the existing units. After my mortgage, taxes, utilities, and other expenses are paid off each month, I bring in over $6,000 in profit from this property alone. It is a cash cow.

The reason it is doing better than my other investments is because it was the best purchase I ever made. Of all of the properties I own, this one is by far the most profitable; I acquired it for well below market value. I have way bigger properties that are worth $5 million to $7 million, and I cash flow less from those properties right now. In the future, those will probably have more cash flow, but I have a partner. So, we're splitting it fifty-fifty.

When you're trying to buy your first property without partners (except a spouse), take the best deals for yourself. One deal that you own 100 percent of can change your entire life. If I decided to shut my business down and live in a cheaper state, I could live off $6,000 a month for the rest of my life and retire! Think about that! Just off of one property!

If you find a great property which stands out among the rest, then do whatever is necessary to come up with the money. Get the best financing terms available and figure out a method to get it closed by yourself. Take the risk and do it if the deal's good enough.

The property I purchased, at the price I paid, could have been sold the day after for a $200,000 profit. Therefore, I knew without a doubt that I would make money from it. So, I found a way to purchase the real estate without any partners. I put down about $200,000 (30 percent down), and I got a construction loan where the lender was able to lend me all of the $400,000 construction costs plus the purchase. So technically if you look at my down payment on a loan-to-cost basis, my actual percentage down was 18 percent down.

If you're looking for a reliable source of income, something that will continue to generate money even when you're not actively working, this is it. If you are fed up with your job and don't want to keep taking orders from other people, owning and managing multiple rental properties on your own (with the help of a team) is the way to go.

Owning multifamily real estate is a 401k on steroids. When you own at least one to two multifamily properties for ten to twenty years, the rents and your equity in the property will grow significantly with compound interest. A property that you have owned for more than ten years will always spit out cash flow, whereas a 401k is slowing burning away as you get into late retirement.

And when you've gotten to this stage, it might be good enough for you. I have a lot of clients that are small mom and pop owners in San Diego. They have a couple of properties from which they cash flow six figures a year from them, and they're fine. They're okay with that and living comfortably. That's all they need and they don't want to do anything else. They just want to chill, travel, relax, and live a simple life.

Some people want to keep building and growing. And if you're that kind of person, the rest of the book is for you because I want to show you how to keep growing, how to keep building, and how to grow generational wealth. The way to do that is to take all the profits that you're getting from your properties and reinvest it as fast as you can.

I cash flow over $25,000 a month from my properties after the mortgage is paid but I haven't taken a single dime of that cash flow because I want to keep building and growing. Now, the caveat to building and growing is that it's a lot of work. It's actually tougher to achieve financial freedom if you want to keep growing to higher levels because you have to use that cash to reinvest and buy more properties. So spending the cash that comes in is the way to keep scaling and building your net worth. Now you can see why I mentioned that you have to sacrifice more if you want to get to higher levels.

And you'll need to keep refinancing your equity, selling properties to get your money out, and buying bigger properties. You'll have to make exceptional decisions over and over. And when you're doing that with your properties, your cash flow gets significantly lowered.

My cash flow fluctuates a lot because I'm selling and buying properties constantly. I'm doing 1031 exchanges into larger assets, which is a tax deferred exchange where you can sell a property and defer capital gains and buy a bigger property.

I'll mention more in later chapters on how to do that. But I really think that if you are looking to truly grow and build very quickly, you have to sell, you have to refinance, you have to not take your profits, and you have to keep reinvesting it over and over again because that's how compound interest builds.

This is why having a high-income career to pay your bills and to be able to keep investing is critical. This is why I keep preaching the opportunity to make millions of dollars as a multifamily real estate agent.

Maybe you're thinking to yourself that if you don't bring in cash flow, then you won't be financially free. That is true. But do you want to keep working and advancing quickly? Or would you rather slow down, relax, stop your job, and be done? The choice is yours. Either path is fine. You just have to know yourself. If you want to take private jets every time you travel, then it's going to take much longer for you to become financially free than someone who is okay with living in a studio apartment in the Midwest who never wants to travel.

Real estate is a great way to call your own shots. If you're fed up with your current job but have managed to acquire a few rental properties or partner with other investors, you can pull in enough income from those investments to cover your living expenses and quit immediately. An example of this would be if you earn $6,000 to $7,000 a month through rentals while only spending $5,000 on living costs. Then you can finally say goodbye to the nine-to-five grind.

But what's amazing about real estate is that it works harder than you ever will. It works twenty-four hours a day, it's always spitting out cash flow on the first of every month. If you quit your job and that cash flow supports your living expenses, you'll have the opportunity to chase a different career or a different passion project that'll bring you income—and you'd be working for yourself.

I don't care who you are; if you're reading this book, you have a purpose to be your greatest self to the world. If you're at a job that you hate, that you dread going to every single day and you watch the clock and you can't wait to get out of the office, then there's a 110 percent chance that you're not living out your purpose.

The beautiful thing about real estate is that when you own rental properties, that cash flow can come without it having to take up a lot of your day—maybe an hour to two hours a week maximum. It's even less than that if you have a property manager; then you have the freedom to create a second source of income. Money is no longer a stress factor for you. And when that goes away, beautiful things happen. Your creativity rises, your mood rises, and you actually want to get up in the morning. You don't mind working long hours when it's for yourself and doing things you love.

I feel fortunate that my life's work is in the realm of real estate. My purpose is not to build wealth through real estate, but it is to help others achieve financial freedom and live their best life. Seeing people fulfill their dreams brings me more satisfaction than anything else. When one of my agents recently closed their first deal because of my mentorship, it was more satisfying than me closing my first deal in 2019.

The money I earn from selling properties and helping clients acquire new ones is why I can continue growing and expanding my portfolio while following my purpose. I love my current career, or my "job," if you choose to call it that.

I now have eleven agents I hired that I train and help on a daily basis, and giving back to people in that way has made me love my career even more. That's what sparked my entire journey to build my personal brand and to help people do what I've done because I know that if I can do it, anyone can do it.

That's why I'm so enthusiastic about helping you to achieve financial freedom with no strings attached, as you will have complete control over both your time and decision making. I consider myself fortunate because I can create new relationships while doing what I love. Sure, one of my goals is to have more properties and more units, but it's not my biggest one.

If I was someone who hated real estate and wanted no part of it, I would buy a couple properties as soon as possible to build cash flow to support my living expenses, then hire a team to do all the work for me (covered more in depth later). This would free me up to pursue other projects. For example, if I loved videography, I would try to become a movie producer or have a media company. If you love music, maybe you want to make music and become an artist and try to chase that career.

The point is that with real estate, you can be freed from your work day that you probably do not enjoy right now. If you are at a dead-end job, have trouble waking up in the morning, get an extreme case of the Sunday scaries, and feel empty inside, you know what I mean.

Do you know why most artists fail, why most businesses fail, why anyone fails? The biggest reasons why is due to a lack of money coming in each month. So if you have money coming in consistently on a monthly basis and money's no longer a factor in your failure, then your chance of success is going to go way up because you now only have to focus on your one thing, your passion.

Think hard about this for one moment, and try to write it down if you can…. If you had all the money in the world, and it was no longer a problem for you, how would you want to impact the world in a positive way? And please don't tell me you would retire and sit on the beach all day. You would feel even more empty inside and bore yourself to death.

I used to think early retirement was the goal for me until I had enough money to finally go on vacation, and after doing nothing for about ten minutes, I would get bored and want to go do something. If you are doing what you love, and your purpose is aligned with your passion, you are retired. Keep doing that until you can't anymore. So what is your one thing?

This is why owning and controlling your own properties is so important. It's why I keep emphasizing that you have to know who you are, right? Are you the person that loves real estate, that wants to keep growing, or are you the person that hates your current job?

If you want to get out of the system as soon as possible, but you don't like real estate, just use it as a vehicle to get yourself to financial freedom. Regardless of whether you're passionate about real estate or simple investing to get cash flow motivates you, you have to know who you are. And whoever you are is perfect. Everyone has their own journey, everyone has their own path, and I just hope that this book can help you get to where you want to go using the tools I have used to reach financial freedom faster than anyone else I know. How many twenty-four-year-olds do you know that beat the system?

Like the other strategies we've covered, there are pros and cons of owning property by yourself. Let's start with the negative aspects. The big con is that all the risk is on you.

You can't rely on anyone else. If the property is in jeopardy of foreclosure, you're the sole person who will suffer consequences, since you have total control over the decision making and you took on all the risk. The bank won't go after anybody but you.

———

Another con is that you have more responsibilities. From taking care of the property, finding the property, managing the financing, executing the business plan, and overseeing any construction work. If you're managing it yourself, you add to that the leasing, accounting, resolving maintenance issues, dealing with tenant issues, and more. In later chapters, I'm going to show you why and how you should build a team and how not take on most of these tasks.

The pros of owning your own property, as I've already mentioned before, include having true financial freedom. No one controls you; you have no partners, you own the asset, and you make all the decisions for the property. You get all the profits, so all the cash flow goes to you. You're not splitting it three, four, or a hundred ways. It's all yours to spend or reinvest. Every dollar you spend on the property, it's to your benefit and no one else's.

While passively investing or using partners has tax advantages, the tax benefits are greater when you're a sole owner because you get 100 percent of the benefits available from ownership of the investment property. Owning real estate gets you a lot of tax benefits. It's called depreciation, a pretty common tax term. A step above that is using cost segregation to write off the property against your income. More on tax options will be explained in a later chapter.

The opposite of all the risk is that you get all the gains and profits. So, if you buy right, meaning you secured a great deal, and if you made the right moves, you get all the upside, you get all the tax benefits, you get all the cash flow, and you get all the principal pay down. You get everything from owning that asset and controlling it. The only person who reaps rewards is you.

At this point, you're likely leaning one way or the other—passive or active. If you're feeling like you want to grow your investment to sole ownership, I want to share some tips of what to look for when you're buying your first multifamily property on your own. It's very similar to anything else, but I would just be very careful.

If you start by buying a bad deal and owning it alone, there's a good chance you're not going to do well on that property. A bad deal is a property that you overpaid for. If the average three-unit property is selling for $1 million in your ZIP code, you should never buy something for more than that price. You're going to be pissed off, and you're going to want to quit investing or change investment paths. The first deal you buy on your own is very, very important. It can make or break you.

Remember those connections you've made since the beginning of our journey? Use them to your advantage. Double check with your mentors, double check with me, double check with people that are in your circle, and make sure that other people think it's a great deal.

I've made an insane amount of mistakes. When I bought my first property on my own, I really wish I had been more of an expert in construction. Looking back, I wish that I had been better informed when it came to selecting the right contractor when I purchased my first property. With no guidance to help me, I ended up hiring terribly unsuitable people for the job and paying a steep price financially. It was not an easy time in my life, as I lost a substantial amount of money due to their incompetency.

Here is a quick story of the worst mistake I have ever made in my real estate career:

When I first started buying properties in 2020, I ended up taking a huge risk and bought multiple properties. I kept investing until I had almost no money in the bank, but luckily my real estate sales business was flourishing, so I just kept depending on my commissions to push me through this crazy start to my investing career. If something else went wrong, I probably could have gone bankrupt...

So when I initially began investing in real estate, I relied on my clients for contractor and property management referrals because I was new to the investing world. I ended up asking for a contractor referral from a well-known investor in San Diego who I was actually buying a property from because he didn't want to do the construction on this opportunity.

I ended up buying that property from him and while we were in escrow, he said that his contractor could do the work for $60,000.

My eyes got wide, my chest started pounding with adrenaline, and I said, "Only $60,000? I will hire him ASAP!"

Massive lesson from my mistake: if something seems too good to be true, always be extremely skeptical and ask the right questions to sniff out the BS.

So I ended up hiring him to complete this major renovation on the fourplex I purchased, and I also had him start on three other properties I had purchased in the same quarter. That was four major renovation projects I was trusting this guy I barely knew to complete!

The biggest nightmare of my life started when this contractor named Jose, started doing the work.

Let me summarize to you how each of my projects went: He finished *none* of them, he wasted and spent most of the money on himself. His construction crew had no idea what the fuck they were doing and did everything wrong. They tried to hide major repairs from me, covered a bunch of stuff up, and half-assed everything they did.

On the project I bought from that investor who referred him to me, I gave him roughly $80,000, and he completed maybe $5,000 worth of actual work. My partner that I bought it with got extremely pissed and will probably never do a deal with me again—we went *way* over budget on the project.

Remember Jose claiming he could do the job for $60,000? All in all, it cost us over $250,000!

Luckily, we bought that property for $710,000 and sold it for $1.4 million, so we still came out on top.

Another crazy Jose story: it had been about four months since he started another fourplex I owned in South San Diego (Imperial Beach), and he promised us he would be done in four months.

Well month six came around, and we had an appraiser coming to the property because we wanted to refinance it to pull out some equity and refinance out of our private money loan that had a really high interest rate.

When the appraiser and I met at the property there were two guys there working and they were nowhere near finished! The kitchen was missing countertops, the bathroom vanities were not in, the flooring wasn't finished, and it looked like shit.

I don't know how, but I literally got the coolest appraiser in the entire world on this property, which honestly saved us over $50,000 to $75,000....

He said, "It's fine, Jason. I understand contractors can be tough. Just put the countertops on really quick and just move the vanities and toilets in the bathroom so it looks like the property is fully renovated."

My jaw dropped, and I ended up moving the vanities myself and just put the countertops on the cabinets without even gluing anything for the appraiser's photos.

So what are the takeaways for you from that story?

1. Don't trust contractors. Always get multiple opinions.
2. Don't trust every referral you get. They can turn into nightmares.
3. Learn the construction side before jumping into a project. I knew absolutely nothing about the operations of construction before these issues. I went through the school of hard knocks.
4. Even after making massive mistakes, you can still make money on every deal if you buy at a low enough price.

At the end of the day, this is the most important thing I can tell you: It's okay to make mistakes if the deal was a great buy. So, be very careful on the acquisition. Be extremely picky on your acquisitions and make sure you can build equity immediately. Then, you'll be well on your way to owning and controlling multiple multifamily properties on your own.

Chapter Nine

UNDERSTANDING DEBT AND FINANCING

This chapter may be the most important, and the reason why it's so essential to understand is because debt can make or break your real estate deal. Debt is truly a double-edged sword. If you have too much debt, you'll lose money and your real estate career could end. I've seen multiple careers end because the investors were careless with their loans.

For example, a client of mine told me an insane story: He bought a ton of properties in 2007 and was way over leveraged on about twenty properties. He was doing a bunch of condo conversions.

Those were huge in San Diego back in those times. Then, the financial collapse hit, the Great Recession, and every single one of his properties got taken by the bank or foreclosed on because he couldn't pay the loan payments needed to keep those properties.

This guy lost everything. Not only did he lose those properties, but he can never get a loan again on his own because his credit history is ruined forever. He went from a net worth of about 50 million to less than zero in about a span of two years. So yeah, shit can get real really quick.

If you get foreclosed on a property, that's on your record forever. So if you ever get foreclosed on or have something that impacts your credit report like that for life, your investing career is screwed. The reason why understanding debt, also known as leverage, is so important is because most people don't understand how to use it correctly. The easiest definition I can give of debt or financing is that it is the ability for you to borrow money from an outside source—whether it's a bank, another person, a company, or a life insurance policy—in order to make a purchase on something.

In each of those instances, it's just you borrowing money from someone and paying them an interest rate or a specific return on their money in order to use that money and put it to work. Say you're buying a million-dollar property. Most people buying their first property don't have a million dollars in the bank, so they put 10 to 25 percent down, and they borrow the rest of the purchase in the form of debt from a bank.

But debt isn't always a bad thing. Real estate is the most stable type of investment that allows you to use debt. Banks love financing real estate, but banks do not like financing stocks or businesses nearly as much.

There's a reason why banks like to give loans to real estate investors or to real estate buyers. The big banks understand that multifamily real estate is the absolute safest, most recession-resistant asset out there. Lending on a stock or a business is ten times riskier than lending on a cash flowing multifamily property with certain guidelines in place to approve the borrower.

I've worked with banks on multiple properties for multiple clients, bought thirty-four of my own multifamily properties, and sold over $300 million worth of multifamily real estate, so I get how these banks think at this point. I've sold office buildings, industrial buildings, and retail buildings; banks always want to flock to multifamily. Banks know that even in the toughest of times, multifamily does the *best*.

In San Diego county, from 2008 to 2010—according to CoStar, the biggest commercial real estate data provider in the world—they only reported fourteen foreclosures for multifamily properties in all of San Diego County in the worst real estate recession ever. They used to call it a heartbeat loan because anyone that had a heartbeat could get a loan. But as you can see from this statistic, multifamily held strong even in the worst time ever for real estate values.

But another important thing to note is how resilient the San Diego market is. There were multiple multifamily markets that got crushed in the 2008 recession, so location is also extremely important.

San Diego has the Navy, life sciences, a strong healthcare workforce, lack of new development, and the best weather in the US. All extremely positive, beneficial factors for real estate investors.

The biggest benefit of getting a loan from a bank is that it significantly increases your return on your equity, which means that whatever money you're putting in, you're getting much more for it. So let me give you a quick, easy to understand example. You buy a $1 million property and you pay all cash for it, so you are out $1 million from your liquidity. Let's say you invest nothing further into it, and you sell the property for $100,000 more, $1.1 million, a year later. You made a $100,000 profit (not including real estate agent commissions and closing costs). You made about a 10 percent return in that period. That's not bad, but not great.

Now, say you bought that same property, but you only put down $100,000, and you got a loan for $900,000 from a lender to buy it. When you sell that property for $100,000 profit net in your pocket, what's your return? You just made 100 percent return because you doubled your money! You put in $100,000, financed the rest, and you ended up with $200,000 after selling the property. That is an amazing return. This is probably the second most important determining factor on how I built my wealth so quickly. My partner and I bought a lot of real estate quickly, and the way we did that was through a lot of private money.

If you don't know what hard, or private, money is, it means that you're borrowing money from a group of private investors. Typically the actual lender groups individual investors together into what is called a fund, and they lend to borrowers (real estate investors) from that fund compiled of investors who want a stable 9 to 10 percent monthly return from the debt fund.

There are pros and cons to hard money. The pros are that it allows you to get really high leverage, so it allows you to put very little down to buy properties. The con is the interest rate is much higher.

As I write this, interest rates for conventional loans are between 6 to 7 percent, depending on your credit and the type of property you're buying. Right now, a hard money interest rate is around 11 percent. If you're getting extremely high leverage, it can be up to 14 percent.

The 14 percent interest rate that I have gotten on properties is a second mortgage, that is behind the first mortgage. Having a second loan allows you to get higher leverage, but usually you have to cross collateralize it with another property that you own.

Cross collateralization sounds like a fancy word, and if you use ChatGPT or google it, they will give you a definition that is hard to understand.

I realized that a lot of business lingo that was created long ago in early civilization was created just to make businessmen sound smart and so that everyone couldn't understand it.

Cross collateralization is when a bank puts the same loan on two properties. The reason for this is because it lowers the lender's risk significantly.

If a bank gives you very high leverage on one property and is worried about your ability to pay back that loan, they will put that same loan on another property where you have a lot of equity, so that they are no longer afraid of being paid back.

For example, I was under contract to buy a multifamily property here in metro San Diego and it was a very good deal. It was a $1.5 million property that I could easily turn into a $2.5 million property if I added two units and renovated the existing units.

I wanted to get higher leverage so I could increase my overall return on equity after analyzing the property. Plus, there were over $400,000 worth of construction costs in the deal, so I had to budget for that as well.

So I went to my hard money lender and asked for a high leverage loan. The lender countered me and said they would only lend me the 85 percent of the property with a first loan of $1.125 million (75 percent LTV) and second loan at $150,000 if they could cross collateralize the second loan on one of my other properties with a lot of equity.

A second loan usually gets completely wiped out to zero when a property goes into foreclosure, so this is a huge reason why this tool is used by lenders who lend a second mortgage on a property.

For most private money loans, the interest rate is almost double what it should be on a conventional loan. So it's playing with fire, and you have to really know what you're doing. The only way I would ever recommend someone reading this book should use hard money like I did, is if you're buying amazing, below market value deals with immediate upside—the kind of deals you know that if you buy it for $500,000, you can sell it for $1 million after finishing the rehab. And that is the kind of deal that I buy.

If you're scoffing thinking those deals don't exist, then you are lacking in relationships. It's time to meet more people who control these deals like myself.

I bought two separate $1 million properties a few months ago. Both were fourplexes in San Diego. My partner and I were fifty-fifty partners; we put $300,000 down, meaning we each put in $150,000. The total purchase price was $2 million. We got a loan for $1.7 million dollars from the hard money lender.

So we got $1.7 million worth of debt, and we ended up putting about $300,000 to $350,000 worth of rehab into the property. We vacated the property and renovated every single unit. Then we re-rented it; put on a new roof; and added new electrical, new plumbing, new windows. By the time we were done, everything was brand new. So we were into the property for about $2.4 million after all costs. We put about $650,000 in with our equity, our down payment plus rehab costs.

We sold those properties the next year for a little over $4 million dollars.

Our profit on that one deal was $1.7 million. We took that profit and reinvested it through a 1031 exchange into more properties, which I will explain later in this book (another extremely powerful, little known benefit of owning real estate).

We got crazy offers on those units and we didn't even list them. People solicited us. We actually intended on holding onto the property, but brokers were calling us, asking if we were selling. We said, "Sure, we'll take a look at an offer." The market was hot, we took the offer, and, boom, we got some insane returns.

There are times where it makes sense to hold and where it makes sense to sell. We knew that insane market in 2021 was not going to last forever, and we were right. I am so happy we pulled the trigger on selling those because that buyer overpaid like crazy for our properties. Fast forward to 2023, those properties are worth less than what the buyer paid in 2021.

Don't be that buyer.

What's the mistake that buyer made? They were way too aggressive because interest rates were in the low threes at the time.

Write down this line: you can date the interest rate, but you have the marry the price.

You can refinance the property as rates come back down, but you can't ask the seller for a lower price after you buy a property.

That's just one example of our extremely successful multi-family opportunities. I've done that twenty-six times in the last four years, and I've found the best deals really fast from my relationships, my team, and marketing. It's just been an amazing ride. Utilizing banks and lenders wisely for a short period has allowed that to happen.

Now let's circle back about the bad part about debt. Debt allows you to scale fast and makes your returns way juicier, but if the situation goes south, it can ruin your investing journey. You risk losing a lot of money by accumulating debt.

The more debt you take on, the riskier your investment is. This is why most banks (especially commercial banks) will only lend up to 75 percent of the purchase price, which is called loan-to-value, LTV for short. So if a bank will only lend you 65 to 70 percent of the purchase price, that means you're putting 30 to 35 percent down.

Banks are always trying to protect themselves from having to take the property back from you as an investor. Banks are in the business of lending on real estate, not owning it.

If you pay all cash for real estate, it's borderline impossible to lose money unless you sell for a lower price than what you paid for the asset. You're not going to risk losing the property to the bank.

That's the only way you can lose money—if, for example, you paid a million for a property, the market went down, and you sold it for $900,000. But that's only if you sell.

If you pay all cash for a property, that means you're going to have significant positive cash flow coming in.

When you have positive cash flow, it's impossible to lose money in real estate. Cash flow is the lifeblood of your business if you're a real estate owner. Without cash flowing assets, you're going to go out of business fairly quickly if you're not making a lot of money elsewhere.

Interest rates will play a big part in your investment decisions. Interest rates change due to a lot of various factors—the economy, inflation, politics, and US treasuries are just a few. In summary, interest rates are affected by the market, our leaders, and the economy. So the market is where people buy and sell bonds. A lot of real estate loans are determined by the ten-year Treasury yield, which takes into account the return rate on the ten-year Treasury note.

Right now, as I am writing this, the US ten-year Treasury stands at 3.733 percent. I refinanced a property yesterday and received a quote at 6.7 percent. This interest rate has a 3 percent spread above the US ten-year Treasury yield.

If you want to invest in real estate, you need to be following the treasuries.

In the height of the pandemic, in August of 2020, the US ten-year Treasury fell down to 0.53. This is why we were seeing rates in the 2 to 3 percent range because the ten-year Treasury was so damn low. That's also why there was a flurry of people buying real estate. So that's one way that rates go up and down is the market, people buying and selling bonds.

There are lenders out there that go off other metrics. So one metric you have to remember is the SOFR rate. SOFR stands for Secured Overnight Financing Rate data. Basically it's a broad measure of the cost of borrowing cash overnight collateralized by Treasury securities. This is also determined on treasuries because it's based on the collateral of those assets.

As I write today, SOFR is at 5.05 percent. Banks will lend somewhere between 2 to 3 percent above SOFR. This week, I got a quote for a loan that was 3 percent above SOFR. It was a floating rate. This is for a lot of banks who use bridge loans, or short-term loans. It's called a bridge loan because you bridge the gap between buying it, rehabbing it, and getting it to a stabilized value.

Another important term you need to know when it comes to determining interest rates is called LIBOR, the London Interbank Offer Rate. It is an interest rate average calculated from estimates submitted by the leading banks in London. Banks do use this to fluctuate what their spread will be for lending. So right now, the one year LIBOR is at 5.66 percent; they'll want to have a one to three basis point spread above LIBOR in order to have a bank fund your loan.

The last thing you want to pay attention to is the federal funds rate. This is the interest rate that the Federal Reserve charges other banks to borrow money from them to then lend it out to businesses, investors, or others.

You can easily google any of these rate indicators to stay on top of where the rates are headed.

Banks want to have a 1 to 3 percent spread, based on what they're giving you for financing for a loan because they have to make money. So if they're borrowing money at 5 percent from the Federal Reserve, they have to make money on what they're lending you.

Most banks borrow money from the US government.

Going even deeper into the rabbit hole, you can understand what affects the Federal Reserve interest rate because there are several factors that do that. Every single bank that lends money to investors or to business owners looks at what the rate is to borrow money from the Federal Reserve. Their rate is affected by the changes in the federal funds, inflation, and how well the economy is doing; it's directly caused by the FOMC meetings.

FOMC stands for the Federal Open Market Committee. This is the board of Governors of the Federal Reserve. Right now, Jerome Powell leads the committee, and they meet about once a month. They dictate whether they're going to keep rates the same, lower rates, or increase rates. So that's why a lot of investors look forward to seeing what happens at these meetings because it can drastically affect what happens next in the market.

We've seen them constantly raising rates the last few meetings here, but as of today, they say rates will remain stagnant because they're seeing a decrease in inflation. As I write, their key objective is to raise rates until they see inflation come back to 2 percent. We're seeing the consumer price index (CPI) consistently above that number. They want to get that number down to two. So the Fed's agenda is to keep raising the rates until they curb inflation.

The Federal Reserve raises interest rates to slow down a rapidly growing economy. As an example of this, one can look at the period from 2004 to 2007. At its lowest point in 2004, the federal funds rate was at almost 1 percent flat, and then as the US economy heated up, the Federal Reserve raised rates to 5.26 percent by March 2007. When the market crashed, rates plummeted again, eventually hitting a low of 0.011 percent in January 2010.

What does that tell you? When the economy is booming, officials look to mitigate inflation, as the more money that circulates quickly, the higher the rate of inflation. In contrast, when fewer people are making money and spending money due to a weak economy, the rate of inflation stays stagnant or even drops (deflation).

When money is inexpensive, due to low interest rates, more people take out loans. People become more ambitious and willing to take chances. This leads to an increase in the sale of properties. In 2020, when rates were at its all-time low I saw so many transactions happen in late 2020 and into 2021. It was a frenzy. Now, rates have gone up quickly. The number of buyers that I have looking for real estate has decreased by at least 60 percent.

I could write a whole book about interest rates, but I admit, I am not an interest rate expert. I just follow the graphs and see what's happening. I look at history and read about it, but I am not a published expert in this topic. I am writing this chapter to help simplify some big and scary terms for you.

It took me awhile to understand this stuff, and when I first trying to learn about it, I got a lot of anxiety. I am trying to lower that anxiety level for you.

So what banks should you work with? The kind of banks that you should work with are the banks that will give you the best service and give you access to the most capital. You shouldn't work with the big four banks out there. The big banks don't care about you unless you're worth 100 million dollars. You're just a little ant in their huge company of trillions of dollars they manage. Even if you're a millionaire, you're still a peanut compared to the clients they have.

They work with the highest profile, the billionaire, and the multi-billionaire clients, and unless you have at least 10 million dollars in deposits with their bank, they're not going to give you the best service.

For that reason I really liked First Republic. As I'm writing this, First Republic recently went under and got bought out by Chase. Such a bummer.

First Republic was a small private bank that offered five star service, with exceptional staff and great loans for customers who had a banking relationship with them. They were a bank based on building relationships. That's why I really loved banking with a smaller private bank, and I'm sad that they got bought out by a big bank.

My advice is if you haven't started a banking relationship with a small bank, I highly recommend doing so as soon as possible.

Now, I understand what you're thinking. "Jason, what if I bank with a small bank and they go out of business and lose all my money?" Great question. Before deciding to invest money with any bank, it's important to assess their current financial health. Are they making a profit? What does their portfolio look like? Are customers withdrawing their funds? In an economic recession, if people are recommending the bank and it appears in good standing, then you're probably in the clear.

If they're a reputable bank with a good brand, worst case scenario they're probably going to get bought out like First Republic did by Chase Bank. I would never keep more than the FDIC insured amount in one bank account. The FDIC insurance limit is $250,000 per bank account. I never have more than $250,000 stored in any one bank account for my real estate business. I have multiple bank accounts—over twenty—for my different properties. The reason why I do this is for accounting purposes and to limit the risk of my money being wiped out in case anything crazy happens. Even the biggest banks could technically fail and, if the Federal Deposit Insurance Corporation won't insure a certain amount, it's best not to keep too much money in one place.

If you're fortunate enough to be in possession of a sizable amount of money, it should not be kept in a savings account where interest rates are minuscule—you can get up to 5.5

percent return right now on US Treasury bonds. The cash that is supposedly 'sitting' in your bank account is actually being used by the bank to invest in other ventures such as loans, stocks, securities, and real estate. To ensure the safety of your liquid funds, US Treasury bonds and bills are the best option. It's actually safer than keeping your money in a bank.

If you have an excess of $250,000, even if you have one account, any extra cash should be allocated to your Treasury bonds, real estate investments, or businesses that you invest in. It's more financially beneficial to put your money into something that will make you a larger return than just leaving it in the bank. And, you should only work with banks that will create a positive relationship with you and significantly help you as you grow in your business.

I recently switched to CalPrivate Bank. No, this is not a paid sponsorship. I just want to give you a bank that I work with because I think they're great. They do good work. I've also gotten real estate loans from Axos Bank, Balboa Capital, First Citizens Bank, Mission Federal Credit Union, and Cathay Bank.

I'm a huge proponent for credit unions because they're smaller banks and they will give you first class service. If you get a loan through them, they'll make sure you're taken care of because they care. This loan means something to them.

Now that we've discussed the factors affecting debt and where to bank, you may be wondering how much you should refinance or put down on a property. This all depends on your risk threshold. Like I said earlier, if you pay all cash, that's the most conservative. In an all cash situation, you're never going to lose, but your return is lower and you can't scale as fast. The more cash you use, the slower you're going to scale. On the other end of the spectrum, if you want to be the riskier person, you should try to put no money down—or the least amount of money down—and buy good deals. You've got to know your threshold of risk.

I can't decide for you which choice to make, but I'll tell you this: if you've got very little money, you're young, and you are just starting out, consider taking a bigger risk. You have little to lose, and everything to gain. Huge disclaimer here: like I mentioned earlier, *never* get a big loan on a property if the deal isn't a home run deal.

If you can't make money on the deal day one or make a huge profit after renovations, never put yourself in a vulnerable position. If you need more help on valuing properties and making sure you are making the right decisions, contact me or someone else who is knowledgeable in real estate investing.

One phone call could change your life.

On the other hand, if your business is already making a lot of money, it might be wiser to take out a smaller loan. With 50 percent down, the risk of losing is extremely low and conservative; you can buy a bad deal and still be okay with 50 percent down on a property. But if you're willing to scale extremely fast, take risks—like I did. It's essential to search high and low for great investments, off-market.

You have to ask yourself, if you were to get 100 percent leverage on this property, a loan of 100 percent, could you sell this for a higher profit the next day? And if you say no, you should probably not do that deal. So how much should you put down on the property? It's been my strategy to put down as little money as possible when just getting started and find a great deal. It only takes one amazing deal to build equity and move it into other bigger investments, and to grow and scale.

Think about it. If you get 90 percent financing and put 10 percent down on a million-dollar property and then the property is conservatively worth $1.4 million after you put $75,000 worth of renovations into it, is that actually risky? No. Not at all.

Now, when should you refinance? In the most basic terms, a refinance is getting a new loan and paying off your existing loan. As an example, let's say you financed a property through Chase and you've decided to take out a new loan on the property. Now you're either refinancing the existing loan with Chase, or you're taking out another loan from Mission Federal Credit Union or any other lender you choose.

When people consider refinancing, there are two primary reasons. The first is called a rate and term refinance. This option is simply to lower the interest rate and/or to change some other terms of the loan. You can also switch to an interest-only loan and/or increase the fixed rate for the term of the loan. These options are specific to commercial loans and will be further addressed in the upcoming section on differences between commercial and residential loans.

Usually a rate and term refinance just means you're looking to lower your interest rate. Now, if you're looking into a cash-out refinance, which is my personal favorite, you'll get cash out of the property.

Let's say you bought a $1 million property with $300,000 down and put $200,000 into renovations. The value has gone up to $1.6 million, and you're refinancing the existing loan of $700,000 and replacing it with a $1.2 million loan. That is a $500,000 difference, which goes into your bank account tax free!

Debt is not taxed, so this is not a taxable event.

This effectively means you've taken out your original working capital, paid off your old loan, and obtained your cash back.

So if you put down $300,000 on the property, and the new value is $1.6 million when you do a cash-out refinance worth $1.2 million, you'll have taken out all the capital that was originally invested.

Now that you have taken out your down payment of $300,000 and your renovation costs of $200,000 in the deal, you can reinvest that money and repeat this process!

This is one of the ways that real estate portfolios grow quickly. So reinvest that money, and don't waste it on a Ferrari. No one cares about what car you drive, I promise.

The difference between a commercial and a residential loan is commercial loans are loans used on multifamily properties with five units or above, or for any commercial asset like retail, industrial, office, life science, hotels, and self-storage; residential loans are only used on properties that are one to four units. So if you finance a single-family home, duplex, triplex, or fourplex, you're getting a residential loan.

The biggest difference between residential and commercial loans is that residential loans are usually fixed for thirty years, and it's an amortizing loan, you're paying the principal over the thirty years no matter what. It's a very cookie-cutter consumer loan that's easy for the general public to understand, and that's why it's the simplest loan out there because it has to be easy for the general public to get and to understand.

Commercial loans get a lot more creative, which means they get a lot more complicated. Commercial loans are rarely fixed for thirty years. They amortize over thirty years, but commercial loans can be fixed for three to ten years. Some loans are up to fifteen years, but usually it's three to ten year fixed.

So what happens after the fixed term is over? It goes into a floating rate loan called an ARM, an adjustable-rate mortgage.

So when that fixed term ends, it adjusts with the market's interest rates. That's the main difference. Also, on residential loans, there's no prepayment penalty. A prepayment penalty on a commercial loan means that if you pay off the loan early, you have to pay a certain amount of the loan back in order for the lender to recoup costs.

With a 3-2-1 prepay, the first year you pay 3 percent of the loan if you pay it off, second year is 2 percent, and third year is 1 percent. So if you pay off the loan in year two, you have to pay 2 percent of the loan amount back. On a loan of $1 million, you'd pay $20,000 in extra costs in year two, because that's 2 percent of $1 million.

One final thing with commercial lending is that there are interest-only loans, whereas typical Fannie Mae and Freddie Mac residential loans don't have this option. I love interest-only loans in high appreciation markets, but low cash flow markets, like San Diego or anywhere in California. So if you're in a big city and you're in a low cash flow market, consider getting an interest-only loan. It increases your cash flow, but you're still getting a lot of appreciation, so you're still technically gaining a lot of equity in that property.

For someone who has never financed a property or studied economics, this chapter may seem overwhelming. While I would be remiss not to discuss these topics, I also don't want you to let this chapter stop you. If you come across a term you don't know or an example you can't follow, keep reading.

You never have to memorize this stuff. You just have to understand the concepts. You can google or use ChatGPT to find anything, but I have noticed that Google, ChatGPT, and other people in the business don't simplify this stuff for beginners, so that is what this chapter was for.

Chapter Ten

HOW TO FIND
AND ANALYZE AN
OPPORTUNITY

I n my real estate investing journey, finding and analyzing
opportunities is the most important, most profitable, and
most competitive edge that I've had. These skills are why
I've beat my competition even when they had an advantage.
The way I came to a meteoric rise is finding great properties. It's
an art and a science. It's very hard to do, and most people aren't
willing to do the work. I was willing to do whatever it takes to
find properties, and that's why I've gotten better deals than most
people. I'm going to tell you in this chapter exactly how you can
find better deals than I did or deals that are just as good.

———

Before I dive into the strategy, I'm going to give you an example to illustrate how critical it is for me and my business. The first two properties I bought were in San Diego. The reason why I was able to scale so fast is because these two properties had an insane amount of profit, and I found them in two different ways. One property was from a broker that followed me on LinkedIn who reached out to me and said they had a property coming to market. I made an offer before it ever hit the market and before any competition could come in.

The second property that propelled my success I bought through cold-calling. I was calling owners to see if they had any interest in selling. I called an owner, and he said that his property manager was listing the property and gave me the property manager's number. I went straight to the property manager and said, "Hey, you can represent me. You can make both sides of the commission if I have a chance to buy this property." This property was the epitome of an eye sore. It was in extreme shambles and had so many lists of issues that had to be fixed. But I knew that property could produce unbelievable cash flow by renovating the existing units and adding two units.

I ended up buying two really good deals through strategies that most people aren't willing to do. One is building your brand on social media and on Google, and the other is picking up the phone. So how did I do it? I'll give you five tangible steps to replicate my system in your area.

The first way was networking with industry professionals, which I consider to be people who are around real estate investors. This has been one that's worked really well because if you network with people who are hanging around other real estate investors, you are going to find a lot of great deals and opportunities. Industry professionals are realtors, real estate brokers, people who own property management companies, property managers themselves, real estate attorneys, title officers, escrow officers, mortgage brokers, direct lenders, bankers, trust attorneys, CPAs, and so forth. Network with people that talk to real estate investors as a part of their jobs; you want to make friends with those people. You'd be surprised how many financial industry workers talk to real estate investors, specifically CPAs, financial advisers, and bankers.

There are several industries that serve real estate investors, and you want to know at least one person in each industry. But that's a really long list! So out of these multiple types of professionals, the two people you want to narrow your focus on to start are real estate agents and property managers. These two vendors talk to real estate investors the most. They're in the grind every single day and when they find something, they're going to send it to you if the relationship is strong. Why? Because if they send you a property, they have an opportunity to benefit from it

To go further into this, all property managers have broker's licenses, and all real estate agents are also licensed in each state. So if you let that industry professional represent you in the transaction, they'll make a full commission from the seller. Even though the seller pays the full commission, at least here in California, the property manager or the listing agent has the opportunity to make 100 percent of the commission if you allow them to represent you.

If you are looking to buy real estate but not actively sell real estate for a living, then don't get a real estate license. If you are looking for deals, you need relationships. The best relationships you can make will be with people who are actively finding deals. If you are licensed, finding your own investment deals, and working a full-time job (or you have a full-time business), you're never going to move things forward. You'll have too many things on your plate.

You're also not going to find good deals because other brokers don't want to send properties to other brokers. So if people see that you're doing deals in the market as a real estate agent, you're probably not going to be their first call when they find a good deal. I highly recommend that if you're looking to only buy property, don't get your license. Network with people who have their license, and let them find you the best deals. This is the best way to do it by far. All ten of my biggest investor clients don't have an active real estate license.

However, if you're looking to sell real estate for a living as in a full-time job, then yes, get your license. But if you have a full-time gig going on, whether your own business or a W2 job, do not get your real estate license. It'll be a waste of your time, and trust me, in the long run, you'll not be saving money. You'll be losing money because you will not see the best deals from people that you have networked with and built relationships with. What is the best way to foster strong relationships with people in business? Allow them to make money! Let your agent, broker, or property manager earn a profit, and they will continue to bring you deals. Keep this up, and both of you will benefit.

But, if you do not like your current full-time career or you aren't making enough to buy your first property, I would highly recommend getting your license and becoming a full-time agent like I stated earlier in the book. It's the fastest way to become an investor if you have no money, no relationships, and no experience.

Now that we've covered making industry relationships, my second strategy to find deals is to just pick up the phone. This has been the biggest moneymaker for me by far. I'll tell you straight up, I've found the most deals and built my business by my willingness to cold call. But then again, I'm also a commercial real estate broker, so this might be a little different for you. If you already have money and relationships, I would not recommend doing this. If you are young and have a lot of free time, but lack money or relationships, it is time to start connecting with others. Reach out to people and form new bonds.

To put this into perspective, have you ever made a dollar without there being some sort of human connection? If you generate income, someone is paying you for it. Even if you are working a minimum wage job at Starbucks, McDonald's, or somewhere else; you might not think your job involves any relationships but trust me—it does. A manager who decides to hire you and the company that cuts your paycheck—there's always a relationship involved.

So think of it this way: other people have your money. Go get it. The more contacts you have and the more people you know, the greater chance you have to make money and acquire advantageous investments. So pick up the phone and start making calls.

You have to have a system in place in order to make any sort of headway. You'll be talking to the same people again and again. It's taken me an average of ten follow-up conversations with a real estate investor in order to get them to collaborate on a sale, sell to someone I have as a client, or potentially purchase their property if the price was feasible.

Before you start calling people, I'd highly recommend getting a customer relationship management (CRM) software to organize your leads. Many people use Salesforce, but PropStream and ProspectNow have worked great for me. They're both real estate-centric CRMs and have every single property in your area in their database. You can easily make notes and create follow-up calls right inside the platform. Using a CRM is the most efficient way to keep track of your follow-ups with others. I would strongly advise implementing one to stay organized and on top of things.

Now, I mentioned earlier in the book that you don't have to always talk on the phone. If you don't like talking to people on the phone, you can send text messages or emails. To find people's information, talk to any title officer in your area. Title companies pull properties from the tax record, and they have phone numbers and emails attached to that property record. They can give you an Excel sheet of a bunch of properties that you can call directly for free, at no charge, as long as you give them the business from those leads or if you get a deal.

Title officers make money if you give them the title business on an escrow that you do. So if you are looking to actively find properties and valid phone numbers, make a great relationship with at least one title officer in your area who's a hustler, who wants to see you succeed, and who wants to help you out. They're a great help with marketing and contacts. They're a great source of referral business as well. So make sure you connect with a title officer in your area before you start reaching out to potential sellers.

To be effective on the phone, you have to understand what the goal is. When calling as a real estate investor or as an agent, you want the prospect to give you a price they have in mind and you want them to tell you why they're selling. The first thing you should say when you pick up the phone is introduce yourself by first name and say why you are calling in a happy and enthusiastic tone. Then, from there you want to directly go into your pitch and keep your pitch very short. All you need to say is, "I'm an investor looking in X City for properties in this submarket. I was wondering if you would entertain an offer on your property?"

They'll instantly tell you yes or no. And if they tell you yes, you try to get some more property information from them. Ask them how long they've owned the property, what the rent roll is, what the property is netting each year after all expenses are paid, how many bedrooms and bathrooms are in each unit, and what capital improvements they've done to the property in the last five years.

Finally, you want to ask why they have thought about selling and what price they have in mind.

That should be enough information for you to go and underwrite the property and to see if the deal works for you or not.

If someone tells you no on the phone, try to follow-up every three months. To build the business and be a good investor, you want a follow-up with these owners at least once a quarter. So every three months, ring them back up. Because things change, people split up, people get in financial issues, people get sick, people pass away. When these life events happen, people look to sell. You want to be on the forefront of these things when they happen.

If you are not a real estate agent and you're only a real estate investor, you want to be very direct and to the point. As a real estate agent the call is different. An investor should be very direct, to the point, and get the information right away on the phone. If they say no, there's nothing you can do to convince them. An investment property is typically a family's biggest investment in their retirement portfolio. So you're not going to convince a stranger to sell the biggest investment they own on your first call if they have no inkling to sell.

The next way to source great properties is through leveraging digital marketing. Pay-per-click ads, Google PPC, and Google SEO work very well for finding inbound leads that will call you to see if you want to make an offer on their property. For example, if you make a website called dallascashoffers.com and you build traffic to that website, people will fill out the form you have on the first page with their email, phone number, and property information. They'll see if you'll make them a cash offer.

This type of marketing is fantastic if you have some money because if people are coming to your website, clicking on your ads, and filling out a form, they have to be at least some what motivated to sell their property.

A great way to actively do cold outbound on the internet is to work with an advertising agency to create paid ads marketing. The agency can utilize Facebook, Instagram, and other social media and create a plan for you. A good agency will create what's called a marketing funnel so you can get more leads.

I would strongly suggest enlisting the help of a professional rather than attempting to handle this yourself. Doing it all by yourself can be a time-consuming endeavor and could drag you down a rabbit hole. It's worth seeking out someone with expertise who can provide their services at an affordable cost; this will help you maximize the exposure for your brand. Getting in touch with competent marketers is easy, with sites like Fiverr and Upwork being great resources. That's where I find my people! So, create a profile on one of those platforms and look for a fantastic media partner that you can hire.

You should also work to build your brand. When you talk to someone, they'll want to know who you are and what you do. Brand building is creating a positive association with your company when someone thinks of you. So if someone sees your marketing online, receives a direct mailer from you, or gets your call and looks you up on Google, you want to make sure that your brand looks reputable and legitimate.

So a brand isn't actually a real tangible thing. If you think about an army of people, the people in the army are what's actually real, but the army is just a group of people. Your brand is an army, but it's an army of different characteristics that people associate with you when they think of who you are.

So if you're known for having integrity, being honest, closing quickly, and doing what you say you're going to do, you have a solid brand and reputation because you have a group of positive characteristics that people associate you with when they think of you.

But if you build a brand by not performing, being dishonest, not doing what you say you're going to do, and trying to low ball people to where it's offensive, then no one's going to want to work with you because people associate your brand with something that's very negative.

Building your brand is very important for longevity. If you want to be an active real estate investor in your market for a long time, you need a good reputation.

Having a negative brand and a bad reputation can be detrimental to your business. It doesn't take much to ruin them. One or two errors can have lasting repercussions, as the real estate industry is much more interconnected than many realize. People remember when you make mistakes, and if you mess up a deal for an agent or broker, they'll talk and associate your brand with something unpleasant.

The last strategy to consider is direct mail. This is one of my favorite ways to find great deals. It's also one of the most scalable ways because it doesn't require a lot of your time or effort. Direct mail has been extremely beneficial for my business because not only have I found a lot of great clients for my real estate brokerage business, but I've also found some great investment deals. I found some hidden development opportunities and lucrative commercial buildings through direct mailers. It's a great way to scale your company because you can send any quantity at once, and they're not that expensive.

It costs anywhere from fifty cents to two dollars per mailer that you send to someone's doorstep. Working with a local title officer to get the specifics of owners in your area is known as a farm list. Once you have that Excel sheet ready, you can send it off to your direct mail provider, and they can generate a quote for you. You then get the option of working with a designer or designing the letter yourself to be sent out to those potential customers. Alternatively, the company you're working with can also design the letter for you. I send out letters and flyers detailing what I am seeking and how I can benefit the other party.

In your direct mailer, you should introduce yourself and let people know you are a buyer looking for properties in their ZIP code. Tell them you can buy their property as is and won't ask for any credits. Let them know you want a fair deal that's a win-win and ask them to call you. Direct mail is super simple. All you need to do is find a great provider; have a good graphic designer, or design it yourself if you're good at that; and then just send it off to however many people you want in your market. I work with a great direct mailer agency. Their website is zairmail.com. If you want more information about them and how to use direct mailers, feel free to email me.

Now that we've covered ways to actively market and find properties, let's talk about how to analyze them. To be successful, you have to understand what makes a property a good buy. And there's many different characteristics that make a property a good buy. Finding the property is the first half of the equation. The second half is vetting that property and understanding if it's a good deal or not.

Start by answering the following questions:

- Is it in a good location? How do I know?
- What are the demographics?
- What kind of renters will be living in my property?
- Is there a clear path to growth in this area?
- What is the supply and demand between buyers and sellers and between tenants and available units for rent? Is the demand curve in my favor or is it not in my favor?
- What's the vacancy factor in my area?
- What will my business plan be with this property?
- What can I do to increase the property value?
- How do the sales comparisons look?

These are all questions you should be asking yourself, and if you don't know how to answer them, don't worry, you will be able to at the end of the chapter. I'm going to break all of these down for you.

Let's start with a good location. This is a tricky topic because a good location might be defined differently based on who you ask. Some people might only want to buy and invest in properties by the beach. So anything away from that is not a good location in their eyes. Some people might want to buy locations where it's growing fast, but it's not a good area right now. That's a good location for them. So it's actually a very binary topic.

So ask yourself, what are you looking for in a good location? Are you looking for something that's extremely stable? Do you want something that's high cash flow? Do you want something that's going to appreciate quickly? Because Class A locations—for example, by the beach—appreciate faster, but they don't have a lot of cash flow.

If you go to a Class B or C location, you might not be in the safest location, but you get a lot more cash flow. And if you're in an area where things are gentrifying, you have a lot of opportunity for growth.

As you consider the location, what are your priorities? Are you seeking a return on investment in the form of cash flow? Are you hoping for appreciation of the property's value over time with less maintenance and headaches? Maybe you want to be ahead of the curve and invest in an area that is slated for rapid growth in the near future.

The best way to analyze what you're looking for is knowing what kind of financial situation you're in. If you are someone who doesn't want a lot of headaches and you have a lot of money, I'd highly recommend looking in Class A areas—the best located, the best tenants, and the safest areas. Good examples of these Class A locations in San Diego are La Jolla and Del Mar. Those areas are premier submarkets in my area, but they're also the most expensive. So in those areas, yield, meaning the cash-on-cash return, is not going to be high.

If you're on the other side of the spectrum, if you're look-ing to grow quickly and you want to cash flow and grow your portfolio in a shorter time, you might want to look in other areas. If you are younger and you're looking to grow like myself, I highly recommend looking at Class B and Class C markets where there's a lot of opportunity for growth.

Around me, a good market would be Chula Vista or Normal Heights because those areas are still coming up. There's a lot of opportunity for growth, and finding those areas is one strategy I have used to create a lot of equity.

Chula Vista is a perfect example of an upcoming market because in Chula Vista they're building a $1 billion dollar bay-front development hotel, retail areas, shopping centers, and other attractions to increase foot traffic and make it a more desirable city. Another example is South San Jose because it too is a growing market. It's not the best area, but rents are going up and opportunity exists there. There are a lot of people and companies moving there.

So that kind of segues into the next question: Is there a clear path to growth in the area?

I only buy in areas where there's going to be a lot of growth because that's how I know that my investment's going to do extremely well when I go into a market. And how do I check that? It's actually not as hard as you might think.

Here's what I do: If you google any city or submarket and you look at demographics to see the job growth and average median income, the state or the local government will usually have stats available on how your chosen city or submarket is doing. There's also massive tech companies, like CoStar, that have these stats and so much more.

So if you really want to find all these stats in one area as easily as possible, go to CoStar, sign up for a subscription, and they'll tell you the demographics and the future growth of any market you're looking in. It's the easiest way to find out how your city's going to do or how your submarkets going to increase in value.

If you don't want to pay for CoStar, then contact a commercial real estate broker and they can pull these demographics and data for you!

The key metrics you should look for when thinking about growth are what jobs and companies are coming to the area.

If the number of jobs isn't increasing in the area you want to invest, then the number of people that move there and the wages that they bring in aren't going to increase either. Look for markets where there are industries that are extremely recession proof.

Perfect example is San Diego. SD employs a lot of people in the military and in the medical field, two of the most stable industries for jobs out there. These two industries are probably the two most recession-resistant industries out there because in the worst of times, people are still going to get sick and the US is still going to have a military. So those jobs are not going anywhere.

And what happens when inflation occurs and when wages increase? Rents go up. What happens when rents increase? Your property value goes up because your property value in multi-family real estate is directly dependent on the income of your property. So look for not only growth in your area, but also see if it is going to be recession resistant. There are some markets right now, like Phoenix or Las Vegas, where investors are getting hit hard because we are in a downward market. Supply and demand between buyers and sellers is not in the sellers' favor.

This is something that you really need to understand because if there are a lot of sellers and not a lot of buyers in your market, your property value is probably not going to go up much. Values go up from buyers wanting to pay a higher price than the last person. This is the reason why values in California go up much faster than a rural state like North Dakota. One hundred times more buyers are looking to buy in California.

Therefore, if there is an increase in rental prices and the demand for purchasing properties is high but supply is low, then market values will continue rising. San Diego is an ideal example of this dynamic. Even in difficult economic times, rents are increasing and property values are climbing substantially.

Now the next thing I mentioned is a vacancy factor. The vacancy factor is the revenue you lose from any vacant units in your building due to tenant turnover. So if you have a 5 percent vacancy rate in your market, you want to—at a minimum—have a 5 percent vacancy factor in your underwriting.

The way to underwrite your property is you take the rental income minus the total expenses, but you also have to subtract the vacancy factor. You have to put a vacancy factor in your expenses in order to make sure you're underwriting your property correctly. So after you add up all your expenses; after you add up what it costs to run water at your property, electric, gas, property taxes, your insurance costs per year, property management fees, advertising fees, and repairs and maintenance; after all those yearly expenses are added up, you'll subtract the vacancy factor. Let's say your rents are $100,000, you have a 5 percent vacancy factor. You have to take the additional $5,000 for a vacancy factor out of the gross income in addition to the expenses I named above.

Your $100,000 per year in rental income, minus $5,000 (vacancy factor), minus all your operating expenses is your net operating income (NOI). Take your NOI and divide it by your purchase price, and that'll give you your capitalization rate, which is "cap rate" for short. Cap rate is the number one determinant of value that real estate investors look for when they're buying a property. So let's say your property makes $50,000 a year in net operating income after all expenses, and then you buy the property for $1 million. You bought that property at a 5 percent cap rate. And the easiest way to tell you how a cap rate works is it's the percentage return that you're going to get in cash flow if you paid all cash for the property.

So if you paid $1 million in cash for the property, you're going to get 5 percent in cash flow every single year because you're making $50,000 per year.

Now, your returns are greatly affected by the interest rate because if you get positive leverage, that means your cap rate is higher than your current interest rate. So if you are at a rate of 6 percent right now and you buy a 5 percent cap rate, you're getting negative leverage, which is a bad thing. Negative leverage means that your return is actually going to be smaller every single year on your cash-on-cash return. So be sure you know these rates and watch out for that scenario.

If it's negative leverage, that means your cap rate is lower than your interest rate. If current rates are at 6 percent interest and you buy property for a 5 percent cap rate, you have 1 percent of negative leverage. That means that your cash-on-cash return will be lower than a 5 percent cap rate if you get debt.

Other factors that I use to determine the value of a property, include price per square foot, which is very simple. It's the purchase price divided by the total gross rentable square footage of a property. If you buy a property for $1 million and your property is one thousand square feet, that means you bought the property for $1,000 per SF. The reason why you want to know that is because if every single property in your area is going in between $500 to $600 a foot, you probably don't want to buy a property that's $700 to $800 a foot because that means you're overpaying for that property (unless the rents are just significantly higher on that property).

Another big determinant value that I look at is the gross rent multiplier (GRM). GRM is the number of years it'll take for you to recoup your purchase price. The simplest way to calculate GRM is to take the purchase price and divide it by the gross rents per year. So if you bought a property for $1 million and your gross rents per year are $100,000, you have a GRM of ten. Ten GRM means it takes a rental income of ten years to get to your purchase price. That's a simple way to look at GRM; it's simply the ratio between the gross yearly income and the asking price.

The only thing that matters for GRM and cap rate is determining what you're paying for the property. So if every property in your area is going for a ten GRM, you don't want to pay a higher GRM than what people are paying because the higher the GRM, the higher the purchase price.

So if I take $100,000 × 10 GRM, it's $1 million. If I take that same $100,000 × 11 GRM, that's $1.1 million, so now I'm paying a higher price than what other people would pay or are willing to pay. In short, it means I'm buying a bad deal.

So those are the three metrics I use most. A lot of people use price per unit, but I don't like using price per unit because it gets skewed a lot. When you look at price per unit, it's determined hugely on the number of bedrooms of the property. So if I tell you that the price per unit in North Park, a desirable submarket in San Diego, is going for $450,000 a unit, you still have to ask me the unit mix. A property comprising all one bedrooms versus another with all three bedroom units is going to have a very different price per unit.

For these reasons, I like using GRM the most because it's the one that you can't fluctuate or mess with at all. Because if you look at cap rate and you look at price per unit, you can skew and manipulate both of those metrics to look better than it really is.

Seasoned investors call it "broker underwriting." Brokers will make the cap rate look better than reality by making the expenses slimmer than what it actually costs to run a property—because the lower the expenses, the higher the cap rate. The higher the NOI, the higher the income after all expenses, the higher your cap rate. So because of this, I like to use GRM because you can't really manipulate a GRM. You can't tell me what rent a property is getting and lie to me about it. If you lie about the rents as a broker, you're just blatantly lying to people, and you won't last long in the business.

When considering a property, you should have a clear plan for how it will be used as part of your overall business strategy.

This is extremely important. You'll need to know if you're going to develop the property or just fix up the existing units. Are you planning to add parking? How about adding amenities? Will there be washers and dryers? What about a courtyard or a dog park in the back? What are you doing to make your property better than any others on the same street? This should be the focus of your business plan.

Your business plan should maximize the value of the property and make the tenants as happy as possible. When I'm buying a property, I analyze what I can do to make this the best experience for the tenants. Because if you are obsessed with your customers, which are your tenants, they're going to love your property, and they're going to want to stay. And when tenants stay at properties, they want to pay you rent for a long time. And if you raise rents a little bit a year, they don't mind because they love the property so much.

Vacating tenants, renovating the unit, and leasing the unit to a new tenant is expensive. Turnover costs will eat up your cash flow quickly. It is the silent killer in rentals.

I bought a four-unit property last year that was in shambles, had no amenities, and had no washer and dryers. The parking spots were pretty destroyed, and it didn't have anything going for it. When I first bought the property, I made a lot of changes. I replaced the windows and doors, gave everything a fresh coat of paint, and installed a new roof. To provide more parking space, I removed some of the grass area and poured concrete for two additional spots—making it have four spots in total. Each unit received its own washer and dryer hookup as well as a washing machine and dryer set. The bottom two units even received their own back patios so the tenants could have a little outdoor area with their pets. After all the renovations, it was like an entirely different complex.

I changed the rental experience drastically. What happens when you add features like parking and washers and dryers? Tenants won't just pay top dollar for the area—they'll stay for a long time. If they have a place to park their car, a place to do laundry, and a nice yard, why would they want to go anywhere else if it's already at a fair price? People only move away if they don't like where they live or something major has happened in their life. So if people are leaving your property, it's because they don't like your unit, the area, or your service. You can control two of those. So make your tenant have the best possible experience, and you'll profit more from owning real estate.

Prior to investing in a property, it is important to have detailed sales comparison reports that allow you to compare the properties current asking price with what similar ones are selling for. This will ensure you don't overpay for the property; after all, the quickest way to lose money in real estate is by paying too much for something. As they say, "The money is made on the buy." If you do not have access to such information, reach out to your contacts and see if anyone can assist you. We are happy to be a resource for you.

All the best real estate investors understand that the money is made on the buy.

For instance, two people buy the same four-unit property in San Diego for different amounts—let's say you pay a million and I pay $800,000. If we then sell it for the same amount of $1.1 million one year later, I will have made an additional $200,000.

The two fastest ways to lose in real estate is buying too high and getting too much leverage, as in too much debt. If you get too much debt and you buy high, you're probably going to lose. So it's important to be smart with your finances in order to avoid financial troubles. I discussed this further in the previous chapter, where I suggested being smart when taking out loans and credit lines. Make sure you're getting a good deal on what you buy; one way of doing this is by researching sales comparisons and trends.

If nearby ten-unit buildings have just sold for three million dollars, why pay more? Listen to the advice of your broker, but never exceed the prices set by comparable sales. If your property generates lower rents, has fewer amenities, and is in worse condition than the comparables on the block, make sure you stay below that price. You should always aim to buy below the sales comparisons. And you should try to pay a lower price per square foot, the lowest GRM, and the highest cap rate for every property you buy in your area. You want to be the lowest paying buyer, not the highest paying buyer. That's how I've made a ton of money on my properties.

An example, just to end the chapter on a great lesson, is on your first deal, make sure you're buying a home run. The first property I bought made me a millionaire. I bought it for $995,000. It had four two-bedroom units that I completely renovated and turned into brand new units for only $150,000. After I rented every unit for $2,500 a month, I sold it for almost $2 million six months later.

That's the kind of property you want to buy when you buy your first property. They're out there because that's just one example of many properties I've found over and over again. Using this strategy works and will get you out of the system. There's a way you can keep doing it over and over so you can scale. I'm no one special, so you can do it too.

Chapter Eleven

THE HIDDEN TAX
BENEFITS OF OWNING
REAL ESTATE

B y now, I'm sure you're aware of the financial benefits of owning real estate. You have cash flow, you pay off your mortgage each month with your rental income, and your asset value appreciates over time. But, there's a hidden benefit that no one ever talks about because the ultra-wealthy individuals don't want you to know this: owning real estate allows you to significantly lower your earned income so that you can pay much less in taxes in April. Owning real estate has absolutely incredible and significant tax benefits. I will explain it to you with just a few examples after I define some basic terms and on how you can use this for yourself. I also want to say you should talk to a CPA about your specific situation. This chapter is only meant to give you information based on my own experiences. Consult your own legal, tax, and accounting advisors. I am not any of those. This is not legal tax advice.

I'll illustrate the definition of depreciation in layman's terms because Google will give you a definition that's very confusing. When I first started in real estate, I was very confused because people call the tax benefits of owning real estate "depreciation." It's called depreciation because the IRS has a rule in the tax code that your residential property or your multi-unit property will become obsolete in 27.5 years. So since the IRS basically states that, you are allowed to write off a certain portion of your building every single year over 27.5 years. The IRS knows that you have a building that's depreciating over time, not in value, but in condition. As time goes on, a roof gets old, the stucco or the wood siding on your property gets old or eaten by termites, windows leak, kitchens get outdated, and your HVAC wears out. All these items on your property depreciate over time.

Something you want to note is that you cannot use the depreciation benefit for land. You can only depreciate the building value. If you own a vacant plot of land, there isn't a building sitting on it that's slowly becoming obsolete, so you don't get any tax benefits. To properly use depreciation benefits you'll need to buy a property with a building on it, whether it's a house, a fourplex, an eight-unit building, a warehouse, or other place.

Here's the basic way to calculate your building value versus your land value: My CPA told me, Let's say you buy a property for $1 million. Use the eighty-twenty rule to estimate your land value from your building value. So if your land value on a $1 million property is $200,000, because 20 percent of $1 million is $200,000, your building value is going to be $800,000. Since the US government sees that your building of $800,000 is becoming slowly obsolete over 27.5 years, you want to divide $800,000 by 27.5, and that brings me to $29,090.91. From the passive income that you get from your property, you can write off $29,090.91 every single year through what's called straight-line depreciation, which is the equation I just showed you.

Very simple, but it doesn't just stop there. There's also many other things you can write off. Many people don't know that if you do construction, you can write off the construction costs of your property. So when you depreciate an asset, basically you're writing off your total basis into the building. And what I mean total basis is if you buy a property for $1 million and you put in $200,000 to renovate it, your total basis in the building is now $1.2 million.

A beautiful thing about that is, even though you think money's coming out of your pocket, it's a write off. But money's not coming out of your pocket and doing nothing. You're investing it into the property, and when you invest money into the property the building value goes up. If you buy a four-unit building at $1 million, and you put in $200,000, you can now write off that $200,000 you put into the building. Not to mention your building value probably just went up to $1.6 million if you bought a good deal with upside. If you're putting in money for construction, you better have bought a property that's going to go up in value by at least 20 or 30 percent.

You can also get tax credits if you build affordable housing. This book isn't focused on development, but if you put money into building more affordable homes for your community, talk to your architect or a city planner about any potential tax credits or tax benefits that you might get for building housing for low- to medium-income people.

But wait…it gets ten times better. I just talked about straight-line depreciation. You can write off about $29,000 a year over 27.5 years with straight-line depreciation. There's something that's called accelerated depreciation. It's very different from straight-line depreciation because in accelerated depreciation, also known as cost segregation, it gives you the ability to write off a significant portion of your depreciable basis over the first few years of ownership.

I'll give you an example. I bought a property two years ago for $1.1 million, and my total depreciable basis into the property after doing construction was about $900,000. My CPA allowed me to write off about $350,000 of the depreciable basis in year one of owning the asset because of the construction and building value, and I did what's called a cost segregation study with a cost segregation specialist.

A cost segregation specialist is just like it sounds; they only focus on cost segregation. If you don't have this person in your Rolodex or if you don't have this person in your network, again, feel free to email me, and I'll make sure that you have this person's information. I've done this five more times at this point. I've bought a property for $4 million. My depreciable basis was about $2.5 million, and I wrote off approximately $580,000 in year one of owning the asset.

Remember in the beginning of the book I said that I started as a real estate agent, and became a real estate broker, and then became a real estate investor. The huge benefit that I didn't even know about being a real estate professional is that if you are practicing real estate for at least 750 hours per year. If you do that on a weekly basis, that comes out to at least 14.4 hours a week.

Whether you're selling real estate, running a short-term rental, working on property management, or anything else pertaining to real estate, if you're a part-time real estate professional, you have the ability to write off accelerated depreciation outside of just your real estate investment income.

This is fucking huge.

If you're cash flowing $100,000 a year and you have $100,000 depreciation, you don't have to pay taxes on that $100,000 in cash flow. But let's say you're like me and you have a large amount of earned income per year. This is why I keep preaching for you to work in the real estate sector and be an investor: In 2021, I made over $1.6 million in net income. In 2022, I made almost $2 million in net income from just selling multifamily real estate.

I was able to write off most of that income by using cost segregation from my properties to offset my income that I made from selling real estate, and I offset all the income I made in cash flow. Keep in mind though, I didn't cash flow much in those years because I was doing so much construction and renovation. During that time I was just putting all my money back into my properties.

By doing that and by using accelerated depreciation, or cost segregation, I wrote off several hundred thousand dollars off my properties in year one and my taxable income was very, very low compared to what I made. If I didn't own real estate, I probably would've paid over $400,000 more in taxes. Instead, the number was much lower than that. My net income on my taxes for federal taxes was below zero, but I still had to pay

California taxes because they are not cost segregation friendly unfortunately.

Now to bring it all home, these tax benefits are 100 percent legal. There's nothing illegal about what I'm saying. I have consulted with tax attorneys, CPAs, cost segregation specialists, and veteran real estate investors. I've paid a lot of money to get this work done and to get this information so I could give this info to you for basically free.

So how do you get out of the system? Become a real estate agent right now, make money in real estate, and use all that money and invest it into multifamily properties. Once you're invested, write off all the income you put into your assets, and you accelerate your depreciation to write off all of your day-to-day income on your real estate business. That is the fucking game right there. I just gave you the entire secret and runway to financial freedom. I mean, that's how you get out of the system in the fastest way possible. This model of doing business has changed my life. If I was just a real estate salesperson, or just a real estate broker, I would be nowhere close to being financially free, and I'd paying half my income to Uncle Sam.

And if you want to learn more on how to do this yourself, feel free to check out my YouTube channel for free information at @jasonjosephlee.

My mentor once told me and I will never forget it: "You don't become wealthy from the things that you do. You become wealthy from the things that you own." So if you haven't already gotten into the game by servicing real estate investors as a broker, lender, property manager, or whatever it is, do it. Start your own real estate business. Make money, and then invest all of it. Write off all your income. Rinse and repeat.

Chapter Twelve

BUILDING AN EMPIRE TO FREE UP YOUR TIME

R eal estate is a very time-intensive business if you don't have the right systems in place. The one big common misconception about real estate is that if you just buy an asset, you can just chill and let cash flow—hang out at the beach, not worry about a single thing because your investments are making money for you. It doesn't work like that. If you are an active real estate investor, it takes time out of every single week no matter what unless you have the right people and the right systems in place.

So, if you want to free up your time and also be an investor and grow your portfolio, focus on building your team. You need to have a good team in place to build your empire without working forty hours a week.

You want excellent contractors who are capable of either renovating or developing your property. It's also important to have a competent legal team of qualified lawyers who can look out for you and protect you in case anything goes wrong. To guarantee accuracy and protect you from audits, you need an accomplished finance and accounting team. You want all of these members and more to help you solve any problems in your real estate business.

This chapter will explore more of these areas, but the first essential hire to make is a property manager. Having an excellent property manager is crucial to successful real estate investment. Your property management team will save you time, allowing you to focus on other aspects of your investments. It's a common mistake for investors to try to cut corners to be cheap and save money on property managers. Stopping to pick up pennies while chasing dollars is never a good idea.

These types of investors want to make sure they maximize their profit, and they don't understand that time is significantly more important than money. Time is not money. Time is way more important than money. If time and money were both currencies, time would be such a more valuable currency because you can't make any more time. We can definitely make more money. Way too many investors have that mindset of trying to maximize their money but not their time.

Why do we invest in the first place? To buy back our time. Do not get caught in the trap of being a slave to your real estate holdings. Real estate can cause you stress and headaches, just like your current job, if you are a penny pincher. You'll be happy to know that having a property manager doesn't take up a lot of your profits from your property. Let me give you an example of my sixteen-unit building in San Diego that's located just two miles away from my house. My property manager takes care of all the leasing, tenant issues, and any problems or repairs that need to be done. They pay the bills and give me detailed accounting reports for myself and my bookkeeper to review. They're great. And guess how much they charge me? They only charge me 5 percent a month of the collected income.

So, if the property's making $10,000 a month in income, they're only charging me $500 a month to do all that work. It's honestly peanuts when it comes down to the bottom line. If you have a property that's making $5,000 a month, you're paying $250 a month for them to manage 95 percent of the headaches for you.

But, bear in mind that for smaller properties like single family homes with lower rent, the management fee will likely be on the higher end of the scale—somewhere between 8 to 10 percent. Even if your house is bringing in $2,000 a month in rent and you're paying the 10 percent fee, you'd still only be out $200. That may seem expensive, but all the time it takes to manage a property is taken into account when considering the fee.

Look at it this way, do you think your time is worth $200 a month to manage your property? No chance. If you do, great, manage your own property, but you'll never grow. Instead of making a couple thousand dollars a month, I can pay that to my property manager and I can keep doing what I do best. Pursuing deals and negotiating contracts is where I really make the big bucks; managing my assets would take up a lot of time that could be better invested elsewhere. I'd much rather focus on helping my agents flourish and grow JLM Real Estate.

If you really boil it down, I have about 120 units here in San Diego and if I were to manage all those properties, that'd probably take up at least twenty hours a week. So, when you break down the math, it just makes sense for me to have a management company in place.

When building your team, it's critical to understand how to pick the right people for the job because I have had plenty of experience making mistakes in this department. Remember my story about the contractor from hell who almost ruined my investing career when he took $100,000 and ran? So, a bad contractor can make or break your life. Same thing with a bad property manager. If you have bad operations, it will end your investing career.

When I talk to people who have exited the real estate business, I hear the same reasons time and time again.

Why do people leave the real estate business, one of the most profitable investments you can make? In many cases, it's because they've either lost money due to bad purchases or simply got fed up with managing their properties. Either way, a lack of systems and/or wrong purchases are often the root cause. It's so easy to avoid these two mistakes. That's one of the reasons why I wrote this book—to make sure that you avoid those top two mistakes.

Honestly, before you buy your first multi-unit property, you should go ahead and hire that property manager. You want to have a manager in place that you trust before you buy your first deal. The team actually comes before, not after, the acquisition.

Here is a simple plan you can follow in order to find the best property manager:

1. Ask everyone in your network who is a real estate investor or a real estate professional if they know anyone who is a good property manager. If you don't know anyone in real estate, then connect with someone on LinkedIn and/or start going to real estate events in your area.

2. Interview a minimum of your three favorite recommendations. Ask tough questions. Ask them their biggest challenges as a management company, about their fees, and about all the costs associated with working with them. Ask what makes them stand out from the other management companies in your area. Last but not least, ask for five referrals of their current clients.

3. Call those referrals and ask them what they like and don't like about the company.

4. Ask the management company for three to four addresses that they manage. Drive to those properties and see how they are operating. Do the tenants look happy? Is there trash everywhere? Is the landscaping clean or does it look like no one has cut the grass in months?

Do those four things, and you will be able to assess who the best management company is for you.

Once you have your property manager in place, the second person you really need to hire is a great contractor. And the secret to finding a great contractor is this right here. It's very simple.

You can do the same checklist I gave earlier for finding a good manager, but take a short drive and explore the area you're interested in purchasing properties. After ten to twenty minutes, you'll likely come across two or three projects in progress. Pull over and introduce yourself to someone working on the job. If that person isn't the boss or head of the company, get their number so you can call that person and take them out for lunch. Make sure they aren't someone you won't get along with; otherwise it could be an unpleasant experience working with them. Additionally, ask them for three client referrals, starting with the project you found them at.

You want to have a contractor that understands the neighborhood; that's why you want to drive that neighborhood you're buying in. The second step is to contact the owner directly or ask the contractor for their number. If they are having any problems and dealing with a stressful situation, or the costs are unnecessarily high because of additional changes to the contract, you don't want to hire them. That way, you can avoid any potential headaches during the job.

Be sure to speak with at least two or three references who have had recent experience with the contractor. What they experienced a few years ago could be different from what you would go through now; contractors can be very unreliable. Thus, it is important to get current testimonials before making any decisions.

Your experience with this contractor's rehab probably won't be the same as someone who had it done years ago. When it comes to picking a contractor, you should ensure that they are currently engaged with active rehabs. Contractors can become overloaded when they get too busy and their service can suffer greatly.

A lot of contractors are tough to deal with, some are slimy, and some of the people will screw you over (especially if they sense that you are new). This is what happened to me. I was a twenty-three-year-old kid trying to boss these contractors around, and at the beginning, I had no fucking clue what I was doing. So they came for blood. They tried to overcharge me on everything, picked the cheapest materials, and took forever to get anything done. I was their lowest priority customer. They probably hated working for someone over twenty years younger than them, so I get it. Once you find a good crew, don't let them go. Treat them well and reward them for doing a good job.

The next step is to build a team of professionals that can help keep your investments on track. For legal services, you need to get a lawyer or an attorney who specializes in real estate law and eviction law in your area. They will be able to advise you on the best way to handle any tenant issues that arise, as well as draft and read contracts when necessary.

On the financial side, it's important to hire a bookkeeper or accountant who can prepare financial statements and ensure all of your taxes are paid on time. Your accountant can also set up systems so that you have an organized record of all transactions related to owning rental properties.

I made the mistake of not hiring a bookkeeper for my real estate brokerage business and real estate investment business soon enough. This is the side of real estate I hate most, and I should have outsourced this way sooner. Outsourcing has saved me so much time and allowed me to do more of the activities I enjoy doing in my business. My door is always open for referrals if you need one.

Now it's up to you. Hopefully you learned something from my hard-learned advice and know when to make your first hire.

You should keep hiring more and more people if you see yourself spending more time on your properties than you are spending time with your family or doing what you love. If you have a full-time job and now you just hired yourself into another full-time job, it's time to delegate.

If you're reading this book and you're a full-time employee or you have a full-time business and that takes up all your time, don't be scared. I promise you, you can invest passively as a limited partner with me or through someone else who has a good track record. You can also be actively investing in owning 100 percent of your deals and not spending that much time on them, if you have the right people in place before you buy your first property.

The biggest investors in San Diego I've interacted with all have their own dedicated management firm, legal team, contractors, and accounting department. The huge owners have all or most of their departments vertically integrated within their company. I had lunch, when I was in college, with a billionaire investor here who has no partners and he owns over five thousand units in Southern California and Hawaii.

The first big takeaway I got from that lunch was that you need to learn how to build a business if you want to be that big of an owner. He has an amazing operation and everyone who works for him are killers.

The second biggest takeaway I got is the power of compounding. He owns every property 100 percent, and he has been in the game for over forty years. He told me that he buys in all markets and he always 1031 exchanges or cash out refinances to grow quickly. I'll talk about that more in the next chapter.

You might be asking how I landed a meeting with a billionaire investor. I played the student card. I had actually called him on his two-hundred-unit property in East San Diego, and he said he would consider an offer if I brought a buyer to him.

After that, I decided to tell him that I was still a student at San Diego State and would like to buy him lunch. He said yes.

That is one huge benefit of going to college. Everyone wants to help you. Once, you graduate, not so much.

Investors like the one I met in college hire in-house employees that work for them full time, because they understand that once you get too big, it's hard to have outside third party contractors handling your stuff. Once you get too big, you have to have a lot more control and power over the people that manage your stuff.

Once you get to the point of owning a couple hundred units, the cost you pay for outsourced property management becomes more expensive than just having your own company.

Operationally it also makes more sense to have your own management company because you will outgrow the ones you use and your team that you have on payroll will care much more about your properties than third-party managers.

Also, when you have your own in-house operations, large investment companies and family offices will take you more seriously when trying to raise money. So if you really want to scale fast with investment capital, being your own asset manager is important.

One of my clients has such a well-designed system that he is only working thirty minutes each month on his business. For the remainder of the time, he is spending quality time with his family and enjoying leisure activities such as golfing or traveling. He still manages to generate over $100,000 in cash flow every month. He's kind of vague about it, but with the amount of units he owns and the amount of equity he has, I know he is cash flowing at least $1 million to $2 million a year.

Switching gears, let's get to another very important point if you're desiring to be a top investor in your market: you have to have a great reputation. If you don't possess a good reputation in your chosen market, I guarantee it will be challenging to expand your business.

This is especially true in the small niche of multifamily investment real estate; news travels fast and far. The San Diego market is a large real estate market compared to most cities in the US. Yet if an investor screws over a broker or cancels an escrow for no reason, everyone hears about it. People like to gossip, and word gets around fast.

It doesn't matter who it is, every investor that has come and gone in this market have the same things in common, which are that they like to take advantage of people and they never keep their word. If you want to be respected and grow your business, it's actually very simple: be easy to work with and stay true to your word.

I don't know how many times I've heard an investor say, "Hey, I'd like to purchase this property." Then they go into escrow and without any justification they cancel. After that point, they will never receive a deal from me again.

It's just crazy to me how much it happens, but it makes sense now. Having worked hundreds of deals, I've learned that experience makes a huge difference in real estate investing. That's why the top 1 percent are so much more successful than the other 99 percent. They do good business, know how to treat people, and understand how to keep their business growing.

The most important relationships for any real estate investor are with brokers, since it's the deal that matters.

Once you get a good deal, there's many ways to make it work. From there, it's just a matter of procedure. Make sure you have an effective system in place, find a competent manager, contract with an experienced contractor, and assemble a dependable team if your project is especially large. But if you don't have a deal, you don't have anything. If you don't have access to deals, no matter how much money or staff you have, you won't be able to make successful investments.

So, who has all the best deals? The top brokers in your market. Make sure these people know how much you value them: take them out for dinner, host a broker appreciation event, and send them cards during the holidays. Cherish those broker relationships. Make sure you treat them well and show them you care.

Not many people are doing this. I know maybe two investors who actually show a lot of appreciation for brokers in our market here in San Diego. This tip I am giving you will definitely help you stand out.

You have to realize that the top brokers have many buyers they can call, so why would they call you first?

Chapter Thirteen

EXIT AND GROWTH
STRATEGIES

As time goes on, property values go up no matter what. I constantly ask investors this question: If they look back at a property purchase they made ten or twenty years ago, do they regret it? Do they wish they had bought more? And without fail, their reply is always something along the lines of "No, I don't regret it. My only regret is that I didn't buy more, as I was afraid the market might take a dive."

My main point here is that when you're investing in real estate, look at it as a long-term investment. Just like stocks or any other investment, if you hold long enough, you will do just fine. And with real estate, not only is your property appreciating over time—so you're getting that appreciation just like any other investment—but you're also getting such significant tax benefits and significant cash flow along the way, even if your property doesn't go up in value. Let's say you bought a ten-unit property for $500,000 in the middle of nowhere in Iowa (or any rural area where property values don't go up much at all). You got a loan of $400,000 to finance the investment. If you pay that loan off over thirty years, you just made $400,000 in thirty years of equity even if the property didn't go up in value and your tenants paid that off for you

Now, in areas like San Diego, values go up considerably. If you hold a property in San Diego and you paid a $2 million loan off over thirty years, you just made $2 million over thirty years, and your property is probably worth over 6 million in year thirty because you bought in a great location. Yes, you paid interest on your loan, but your tenants paid that interest for you because your property's not sitting vacant. That's the biggest difference between a single-family home that you live in versus an investment property.

On your single-family home, you're paying the mortgage, maintenance, landscaping, trash bill, water bill, electricity bill, and roof replacement bill, when that time comes. But when you own an investment property that cash flows well, your tenants pay these costs for you and they pay the loan down. Your tenants are paying for everything. And when your tenants pay your loan down over thirty years, it is powerful compounding.

If you invest wisely by taking out a $1 million loan to purchase an income-generating property, you can become a millionaire in thirty years if you did nothing else after that. It doesn't matter who you are or what kind of investor you are—if you leave the property alone, collect some cash from it and hold on to some reserves in case of emergencies, you will be worth

$1 million eventually. In fact, if that property is located in a growing location, your net worth could amount to five times as much! The power of real estate is underrated and not explained correctly enough.

If you want to grow your portfolio quickly you should never, ever cash-out and pay capital gains. One really challenging part about real estate is that when you sell something for a profit, you get hit hard with capital gains taxes. It varies from state to state, but often it's 15 to 30 percent of your total gains.

For example, if you net $1 million on the sale of a property, and you cash out of it, you could be paying $200,000 to $300,000 to the IRS and state. It's demoralizing to give away hundreds of thousands or even millions of dollars in taxes. But sometimes people are in need of quick cash, so they have to do it.

You can legally avoid the capital gains and grow your portfolio at the fastest level possible using these methods: a cash-out refinance and a 1031 exchange.

I have talked about the cash-out refinance earlier in this book, but it's so powerful, I have to bring it home with another story.

I asked one of my clients, "Hey, how did you grow your portfolio over the years so quickly?" And he said, "It wasn't quickly, but I did it slow and steady. I bought at least one property a year when I started." Every three years, when the properties appreciated, he would refinance every property he owned and use that money to buy another one. So, eventually, when he had five properties, he just kept refinancing those five properties and buying another one. And then refinanced six properties, bought another one. Refinanced seven properties, maybe bought two this time. And he ended up with fifty properties.

This is the power of buying in a fast appreciating market like San Diego. This strategy would never work in Alabama!

The guy's in his late fifties, and he started when he was thirty. So, I mean, he made some great moves by refinancing his equity and buying more property. And the way he could do that every three years was because his values went up so much every single year. He bought a property by the coast for $200,000 when he first started, and it's now worth $5 million. Imagine how many times you can refinance that property when it goes from $200,000 to $5 million in twenty years. You can just keep pulling cash out. It's a piggy bank.

Refinancing, followed by investing in more properties, allows you to take out more cash and reinvest the profits. This act creates a snowball effect; the more properties you purchase, the more cash you can access. This exact reason is why I think every single person who's looking to grow their portfolio should buy in high appreciation markets.

The second way, which is my personal favorite and what I've done to grow my portfolio extremely fast, is called the 1031 tax-deferred exchange. It's called a 1031 because that's the section in the IRS tax code to which this applies. I'll give you the simple version that's very easy to understand.

As I said, when you sell a property, you have to pay capital gains. But the 1031 exchange was a rule that the US government created. Think about the people who create the rules in our country. They all own real estate. They're wealthy investors.

So, they've made this rule for themselves, and you need to take advantage of it. The IRS Section 1031 Code states that when you sell a property in the US, you can take all the gains that you got from the property, defer the taxes, and reinvest them into a property that is the same price or higher purchase price and where you take on the same amount of debt or more.

So, let's say you sell a property for $1 million and you have a $500,000 loan on it. Now when you buy a new property you have to take out the same amount of debt or more. So, you're going to take that $500,000, get a loan of $1.5 million, and buy something for $2 million.

When you do an exchange, you can also add more funds to the exchange if you want to. So, if you sell a $1 million property, you want to buy a $5 million property, and you have extra cash laying around, you can add more money into the property as your down payment to afford a larger property.

The thing you need to worry about the most when you're doing a 1031 exchange is that you have forty-five days to identify a new property after you sell the previous property.

The latter is called the downleg property. The downleg is the property you sell. You then have 180 days to close on your upleg property, also known as the property you're buying. So, you have forty-five days to identify it and then 180 days to close from the date you sell your property. People often worry about time constraints, but I'll share the secret to extending the timeline. Make sure you work with a broker who knows how to maximize these timelines for you.

One way of doing so is to incorporate thirty-day extensions for your escrow on the property you're selling. If the buyer is completely committed, it can give you another thirty to sixty days to look for your new property and exchange. This way, instead of the usual forty-five days of looking around, you now have three to four months to search for a 1031 exchange. It's much less stressful if you do it this way. All successful investors do this.

There are three types of 1031 exchanges I want you to know about. I'll be very quick to explain these and not make it too difficult to understand. A simultaneous 1031 exchange is the standard 1031 exchange that I just talked about, but the second one is a 1031 improvement exchange. A 1031 improvement exchange lets you take the profits from your sale and use them to buy the property you want to acquire and also set aside a portion of your equity to complete the remodel. This allows you to keep more cash in your bank because you don't have to pay out of pocket to fix the property.

You keep that money with your 1031 exchange accommodator, who holds the funds for you when you're doing an exchange, and you use that money to rehab your property.

This is great for people who don't have that much cash in the bank but still want to grow their portfolio. So, let's say you come out with $1 million in equity to put down on a property, but you don't have money to remodel it. So, maybe you only put down $800,000 on your next investment, and you keep $200,000 with the accommodator to pay the contractor to make that property brand new and stabilized. And that's exactly how you would use the 1031 improvement exchange.

The last type of exchange I will mention is the reverse 1031 exchange.

This one requires a bit more work, but to keep it short and simple, I'll give you the basics. It's exactly what it sounds like. You're doing a reverse 1031 exchange, so you're buying the property you want to buy first with your own cash, and then you sell the property within six months of buying the property that you want to buy. And you get the money and the capital gains are tax-deferred after you sell your property. You're paying yourself back without paying taxes after you buy the property you want, and then you are selling your relinquished property afterwards. The only negative is that there are more fees to this type of exchange. It is more complicated. Some banks don't allow it, and you have to have the cash upfront to do it. So, other than that, the pros are that you have all the time in the world to buy that property you want to buy, and then you can sell your property after you buy the property you just purchased. It's an amazing way to build wealth if you have cash in the bank, and you lower your risk of not finding your perfect exchange property.

Something important to know about 1031 exchanges is that your basis does follow you. Let's say you sold a $1 million property thirty years ago, and now you own a $20 million property. If you cash-out, your capital gains follow you. Imagine you sold that property for $1 million dollars, you profited however much, and your equity from that million dollars is now $20 million—which can happen if you exchange for a long time. If you cash out, you're going to get taxed on all the gains from all the properties you exchanged. So, the goal is to never cash out. The goal is to keep exchanging—swap until you drop is what they call it—and let your kids or your heirs inherit the property and they can sell it tax-free. They can do this because they get a step-up in basis after the current owner passed away and gave the property to someone in their family trust. That's very important to know.

The way I've really utilized 1031s to my advantage is that I've been able to buy smaller properties with little down using my own cash. I've used this strategy to acquire smaller rental properties, such as fourplexes, triplexes, and duplexes. After two years of managing the buildings, I was able to take all of the equity that I made from adding value to these properties and invest it into larger assets.

For example, I bought two fourplexes in South San Diego for $1 million each. I sold each of them for almost $2 million, and I rolled all the profits into a sixteen-unit property by San Diego State. Now I own a sixteen-unit property in a prime location that's cash flowing significantly more every month.

I found a triplex and a duplex from my broker relationships I have made here in San Diego, and I sold those properties after two years for a $1.5 million gain, and I bought a trophy eleven-unit property in Pacific Beach for $4.8 million. That is the power of the 1031 exchange.

In two to three years, I will exchange that eleven-unit property for a twenty-unit building somewhere else in San Diego County.

By now, I hope you recognize the financial potential of working and investing in real estate. It's unlike anything else. Before you take your first steps, I want to reassure any readers who may feel anxious or uncertain. After all, I've personally worked with hundreds of people just like yourselves—those who harbored doubts and held little knowledge of real estate. This book was written to erase all your worries and equip you with the tools necessary to begin your investment venture. If you just refer back to this book, you can be a successful real estate investor without buying another course or program. I put all the strategies I use in this book. All you need is a mentor to help guide you and keep you accountable.

If you don't need a coach or a mentor to keep you accountable, then go kill it on your own. The goal is to make new relationships. If you do that, you will be successful.

If you reach out to me, I'm happy to help you. I'm happy to be that source of information for you. But the only way to change your actions is to change what you input into your brain—the knowledge.

What you learn affects your beliefs, and when your beliefs change, so do your actions.

When your actions change, you start achieving goals you never thought was possible.

My goal for you is to be a successful investor that has all the time in the world. I want you to defeat the matrix, so that it's up to you how you want to spend your time. You're the one who decides. You can choose when to take days off, work, or go on vacation—whenever suits you best. I want you to have properties that are giving you passive income every single month, like a lottery machine.

I will never forget one of the first lunches I had with one of my clients who is a big investor where I live. He said, "Jason, on the first of every month I feel like I'm winning the lottery! I have tenants paying me cash every month, and I don't even do anything. It's crazy!"

I hope this helped you or at least opened up your mind to the possibilities of life.

Anything is possible if you set your mind to it. So, go out and get your own wealth because the wealth is created by you. Whether you end up rich or poor, it's your fault. It's all on you. Stop making excuses. Life isn't fair.

It's more gratifying to earn your success than to be born into it. Therefore, go out there and pursue your dreams, make your own destiny, and become self-made.

—Jason

ABOUT THE AUTHOR

Jason Lee was born in South Korea and moved to the Bay Area when he was seven years old. From a young age, Jason's parents taught him the meaning of hard work. His mom was always working two jobs, and his father would commute an hour to San Francisco in the middle of the night to work as a security guard.

To help his family financially, Jason tried everything to make enough money. After he found real estate, his career took off. In the last couple of years, Jason has represented over 100 investors and closed real estate deals worth over $325 million in Southern California.

In 2023, Jason's company received the award for the third fastest growing company in San Diego. When he was twenty-three, he was a finalist for REALTOR Magazine's "30 Under 30" list and paid for his brother's tuition at University of California, Berkeley. Currently, Jason's portfolio is worth $50 million and comprises of over 120 Multifamily units in San Diego County.